THE RETURN OF
Urban Myths

THE RETURN OF
Urban Myths

Phil Healey & Rick Glanvill

Virgin

Dedicated to Frances, Yael and Ollie
and our families and friends (of friends)

First published in Great Britain in 1993 by
Virgin Books
an imprint of Virgin Publishing Ltd
332 Ladbroke Grove
London W10 5AH

ISBN 0 86369 752 6

Cover illustration and text illustrations by Phil Healey

Phototypeset by Intype, London

Printed and bound in Great Britain by
Cox & Wyman Ltd, Reading, Berks

acknow*ledgements*

Firstly, especial thanks to the apparently very thirsty urban mythologists John and Sarah Hartwell, and Jonathon A. Salt, for their letters. We also really enjoyed and appreciated the contributions of correspondents David Bonney, John Boyd, Gez and Penny (the basket Caseys), Ian Cassidy, Steve Collier, J. Glyn Davies, Andrew Denny, Paul Gallagher, Jon Harris, Stephen Harris, Graham Hopwood, Brendan Joyce, Emma Loveridge, David McDonald, Sara Miller, Richard Newton, Dave 'the smell was enough to knock out a bull' Percival, Colin Richards, Lindsay Roberts, Paul Screeton, A.H. Smith, Brett Stevens, Robert Urbanus and Wouter Van Zijc, amongst many others too numerous to mention.

A general showbiz-type thank you to Katie Davies, Les Newman, Christine Williams, Cindy, Maureen and the thousands of other callers into *This Morning* (a lovely programme); Nick Knowles from TVS's *Coast to Coast People*; and that bloke who sat next to us on *TV-AM* while we plugged the book (Mike something or other); also those who jammed the switchboard during Shyama Pereira's show on GLR, and LBC's Derek Hobson and the Robbie Vincent Show (thanks to Robbie in particular for his support of the book) and researchers thereof, as well as our friend of a friend, *Radio 5*'s Danny Baker, for his indecent exposure of our book; yet more thanks to all the various radio presenters on all the stations across Britain who had us on (or were we having them on?); and cheers, mates, to those big down under (!) – Malcolm Elliot, Ranald McDonald (no relation) and Brian Bury in Oz.

Instant gratification to: Tony Ageh, Mervyn Ashford,

Sarah Ball, Paul 'I don't be*lieve* it!' Baker, Albert Becker, Alan Bird, Alan Broadhead, 'Nicolai Ceausescu', Tony Collingwood (see – we never said the underpants were yours), Yael Cohen, Paul Crome, Julie Douglas, Keith Drummond, Deke and John Eichler, Phil 'Mackem' Eccles, Judy Finnegan, Danny Flynn, Emma Freud, the Glanvills, Richard Greenleaf, Stephen Harris, the Healeys, Dave Heywood, Andy Horn, Dave Kimberley, Mark Lawson, Ken Livingstone, Frances Lloyd, Alex MacLean, Ian McCarthy, Richard Madeley, 'Crazy' Kwesi Mansah, Andy Medlock, Chris Morris, Jan O'Neil, Glyn Phillips, Inkington Pinkerton, Dave Powell, Ceri and Al Preston, Q, Mick 'Mañana' Quirke, Monique Roffey, Richard Schram, Satwinder Sehmi, Willy Smax, Wg Cdr Alex Stewart, Mrs Jessica Stevens, Jim Thompson, Mark Urgent, Mark 'Spider' Webster, Tim Woolgar and Steve Wright.

And where would we be without the boundless hospitality extended to us in those excellent hostelries, The Hope in Smithfield and The Three Kings, Clerkenwell Close. (Cheques cashed, coach parties welcome.)

To the other mythologists throughout Britain, Ireland, Australia, New Zealand, Africa, Canada and the USA who got in touch: keep writing – we want to go global.

A sincere Gorbals handshake to Deborah Orr at the *Guardian* for giving us our *Weekend* break.

Also thanks to Sally Holloway, Riona MacNamara, Guy Lloyd, Paul Forty and those smashing press people Marie Reynolds and Charlotte Tudor, and the '*rip-roaring*' sales force at Virgin.

contents

mean *machines*
Spanners in the works
45

A low note; On the skids; Motorway microwave; Tow job; Getting the boot; Hitched up; Eye eye; Cow down below!; The driver's seat; Whiplash effect; Slip road; A nasty set-to; Caught in the headlights; A lot of bollards; Mythellaneous

the long *arm of the law*
Scams and scamsters
63

Signed, sealed and delivered; Return to sender; A matter of trust; Foul play; Crisp business; Fitted-up wardrobe; Take the tube; An unfair cop; The quite good Samaritan; Who guards the guard dog?; Pipe down; Un-Des-irable; Trial by TV; Soled out; A crushing blow; Duvet bugs; Off the back of a lorry; Reds in the Fed; Blue murder; Mythellaneous

food *and drink*
Half-baked hiccups
83

One lump or two?; When men were men; You must be choking; Locust pastie; Frankhurter; Family concern; Gums and plums; Cream tea-leaf; Norra lorra luck; Stake-out; A sour note; Mythellaneous

international *incidents*
Fabulous foreign affairs
97

The Mexican tobacco pouch; Very disturbed; The Aussie flea-pit; Measure for measure; Child hood; When in Rome; Walt's and all; Divine intervention; I wanna be like you-oo-oo; Alone again, naturally; The taste of Greece; Lava's leap; Midnight run; Underground service; Bun voyage; Overnight bags; Hands off; Double your money; Hard to swallow; Kenyan customs; Don't fetch!; Express yourself; A grizzly experience; Heaven scent; Wang end of the stick; Mythellaneous

friends *and relations*
Nowt so queer as folk
125

Phone home; Taking the Michael; Six education; Naïvety play; A Harrowing event; Passing out; Bubble trouble; A friend of the family; Left baggage; A trip out; Home and away; Kitty go home; A smashing honeymoon; Last night; Five-year hitch; Near the knuckle; Take a chance; Privatised depression; Paperboy; Give him the boot; Pole-axed; A last wish; All is not rosy; You can't keep a good man down; Robin red-face; Mythellaneous

campus *capers*
Extra-curricular activities
155

Widen the circle of your friends; Pairs of genes; Watered-down beer; Plant pot; Even pottier; A wee dram; Cough up

surgical *spirit*
Clinical comical casualties
165

Pea soup; Special delivery; What a drag; Floored; Funny feline; From beer to eternity; Nurse knows best; Chomping at the bit; As directed; Superglue cock-up; A strange twist; Getting the point; Snooker loopy; Finger-licking good; Body and soul; A slice of life; Mythellaneous

xxxx-*rated*
Raunchy risqué romps
185

Hold your loved one; Mr Blobby on the job; Rub-a-dub; The unkindest cut (again); The genital touch; Her pedigree chum; Whose baby?; Black pride and joy; Wart a secret; The party pooper; Balls bounced; Potato stew; Massage virgin; Mythellaneous

that's *showbiz*
Stars and tripe
203

'E always calls me that; What a shower; Coping with
adversity; Tip off; Hitched up; Best for Last; Stand-up and
be counted; Oh oh dear; Shanks' phoney; Bridge of sighs;
Going overboard; Last for Best; Quite Frankly; Mythellaneous

occupational *hazards*
Nine-to-five nonsense
219

Super fly guy; A miner tiff; Playing away; The big welcome;
The Navy lark; Para-noia; Capital hideout; The bottle of
Britain; Gull-able; Right royal burial; The missing link;
Highly unrealistic; Trouble brewing; Danger down below;
Broom with a view; Close calls; So re-spectacle; Mythel-
laneous

wanted
240

intro*duction*

Welcome again to the preposterous world of urban myths. In our first book, we set out to catalogue the absurdity, variety and comedy of apocryphal stories currently in vogue at that time. And it proved very popular. *Healey and Glanvill's Urban Myths* was the most comprehensive collection of urban myths ever published. Until now.

At the time we imagined there were a few corkers we'd overlooked, but probably not that many. How wrong we were – as this cult collection of over 200 new and second-hand first-raters proves.

As we freeloaded our way around the country promoting the book, everyone who bought us drinks or got in touch with us would present us with their own variation on an old theme, or have a new story to share, and it became clear to us this was a national obsession.

Then when a flood of letters began to arrive from far-flung locales around the world, such as Australia, Namibia – even Cumbria – it dawned on us that urban myths were a global phenomenon that we would have to exploit further. And here's the result: *The Return of Urban Myths*.

So what is the attraction of these mirthful anecdotes? Urban myths are fascinating, funny or occasionally horrific stories that are told as true but have highly dubious origins. They usually happen to a friend of a friend, someone who is not actually known intimately to the teller, but is a very vague acquaintance. This status is crucial to the suspension of disbelief, because the tales are usually too good to be true, too poetic in their denouements, too sadistic in their vengeance or involve far too many convenient coincidences to bear much investigation.

It would break the spell if you could get on the blower and ask the person involved if they really *did* sit on that Chihuahua and kill it. Then again the story would be nowhere near as toe-curlingly enjoyable if the events happened to a total stranger no one could relate to.

Myths are not rustic folk tales or ancient legends of derring-do. They are tales from the paranoid metropolis, documenting 20th-century obsessions, bigotries, fears and frailties. The fact that many people defend their yarns' validity with vehemence, even aggression, says something about how loudly they strike a chord in us.

Like jokes, urban myths are a release valve, a bar-room prop. They're frequently just as funny, but more moral and often disturbing.

They caution against excess in all forms – vanity, alcohol, avarice and sex (even the 'XXXX-Rated' stories are perversely moral). They place their faith in the experts (up to a point), and chide fecklessness. They fear innovation and social change, animals with attitudes and children with chutzpah, and they distrust anything remotely foreign. In short, they say a lot about our inner psyche.

But the plots are never constant or set in stone. Through the medium of Chinese whispers, they are under constant evolution as the years pass, customs change and fads disappear. One strong theme may spawn many closely related offspring that carry the threads of the original into a new era. The process is carried out by storytellers who customise and enhance them to achieve greater effect.

In this way urban myths are frequently born from the

embroidery of a half-remembered event or unattributed filler in the tabloid press.

One case is quite instructive. When we appeared on ITV's *This Morning*, we were told about a team of ITV current affairs researchers who a few years back were investigating a story circulating about the supposed spate of kidnappings of young children at Disney theme parks. (We feature the story here in our 'International Incidents' section.)

Dozens of phone calls to various people who knew the story produced just a string of friends-of-a-friend of the apparent victims. The newshounds decided to go to the heart of the story to check its veracity.

After an exhaustive investigation (involving the immense hardship of a two-week, all-expenses-paid stay in a luxury Florida hotel), they decided they were on a wild goose chase, and that the story was apocryphal. (Well, we could have told them that . . . and for only *one* week in Florida.)

We believe the same result would follow close inspection of virtually every other modern legend, whether it be the 'spider in the Yucca plant', the 'kidney burglar' or the 'strip-show face louse' themes. Real life and urban myths are mutually exclusive.

But how do you spot an urban myth coming? Judging by the response from those who've seen our first book and our weekly column in the *Guardian's Weekend* section, this is an area of fascination for many people. So as a service to society, here's our brief, friend-of-a-friend's Rough Guide to Myth-Spotting . . .

The Protagonist is always 'a friend of a friend' or 'a mate of a woman at work' or 'my second cousin's second cousin's drinking partner', but never someone who can be named (unless it's a celebrity, in which case it's even less likely to be true).

The Location is tailored to suit the audience, and contains vague local references you might share to lend credibility. If it's a rural setting there are always mysterious country ways about to unfold; if it's more exotic than that, they'll rely on the fact you've probably never been there, so they can be as bigoted as they like and get away with it.

The Plot contains far too many dramatic turns of events, bizarre details, irrational responses, and too much soppy serendipity that subverts the everyday and capsizes life's rituals – stag-nights, holidays, meeting the in-laws or having a brush with the law.

The Pay-off is just too neat. The threads of the yarn are woven together a little too tidily, much like a punchline, and you know you've been stitched up.

Suitably armed and emboldened, we trust you'll sit back and enjoy this second cult collection. Feel free to retell, expand and exploit these stories to your own ends. We certainly have.

urban *classics*

The cream of the crop

These well-honed legends have more than stood the test of time – they've positively thrived on it. Their universal appeal cuts across the generation gap from the nursery to the nursing home. Celebrating a whole galaxy of human frailties, these star stories represent the top of the hit parade of myths: most told, most widely, by most people. Tales you will turn to again and again.

the turkey *trot*

A friend of a friend bought his Christmas turkey from a local farm last year, determined to have a full-flavoured dish for the big day.

He loved his Christmas dinner, it was the culinary high-spot of his year, with golden roast turkey, roast potatoes, sprouts, stuffing and floods of gravy – smashing.

The bloke picked up the heavy, pre-plucked fowl on Christmas Eve. It was so fresh it still felt warm. He bundled the dead weight into his car, drove home feeling especially festive, and squeezed the huge roaster into his fridge as soon as he got in.

The next morning, he woke up especially early to gut and season the big bird. When he opened the fridge door, however, he had something of a surprise.

Apparently the huge bald gobbler had only been stunned by the farmer.

Furious at its frosty captivity and sore at the plucking, it lunged out of the fridge and savaged the hapless bloke, before smashing through the French windows to freedom.

take *a break*

A friend of a friend, out on a shopping expedition, was in dire need of refreshment.

So, laden down with her purchases, she found a cafeteria and bought herself a refreshing cup of tea and a Kit-Kat. The place was so full the only seat she could find was opposite a scruffy punk reading the paper, but she plonked her bags down and relaxed.

Apparently, as she did so, the punk folded up his paper, reached forward for the Kit-Kat, broke off half and shoved it in his mouth.

The woman was taken aback and quite speechless, but the punk ignored her, and a minute later he picked up the rest of the bar and scoffed that as well.

By now the woman was livid. Fuming, she reached forward for the punk's cream cake, took a massive bite, then threw it back down on the table, before gathering up her bags and storming out of the cafeteria.

Still angry, she decided to catch the first bus home, felt in her pocket for her travelcard, and found her own Kit-Kat intact.

an 'L' of an accident

A friend of a friend was taking his motorcycle driving test a few years ago on a local estate of back-to-back terraced houses. It was a grey and drizzly day, and all the dreary streets looked the same.

The test itself involved the learner riding around an agreed circuit. At certain points the stony-faced examiner would be watching, checking certain manoeuvres and ticking things off against his list.

The learner was pretty nervous, but the test seemed to be trundling along quite well. Then the examiner flagged him down and said he was about to test his emergency stop.

He told the biker to continue driving around the streets and at some point he would jump out and shout 'Stop!'

All tensed up, the biker set off round the streets. A few

minutes later he'd completed most of the circuit and the examiner still hadn't jumped out.

Then, when he rounded the last corner, he saw an agitated group of people in the middle of the road. They were gathered round the pole-axed, out-cold examiner.

Apparently he'd 'tested' the wrong bike.

> That one's been around since the introduction of the bike test soon after the Second World War and really doesn't seem to have altered. Even in today's sophisticated society people seem to get a kick out of authority coming a cropper.

flat *season*

A friend of a friend, who is a housing officer, had to rehouse an old gypsy on the ninth floor of a block of flats.

Understandably, the old fellow wasn't too keen, but there was nowhere else for him.

After a few weeks, the housing officer started to get complaints from the old man's neighbours, not about the lift being out of action (as usual), but about a mysterious thudding and scraping occasionally coming from the new tenant's apartment. So the officer followed up the reports and went to check on the noises, but when she knocked on his door, the old bloke would only open it enough to peer out. She asked him about the noises and he explained the neighbours were always picking on him and told her to clear off – or words to that effect.

This continued for a few months. Neighbours would complain about the intolerable racket from this secretive old geezer's flat, and the housing officer would dutifully arrive on his doorstep, only to be vociferously scared away.

Apparently, the old man got so unreasonable that eventually she had to obtain a police warrant to search his flat, accompanied by officers of the law.

When he answered the door, they barged past him to the shock of their lives – neighing away in the middle of the floor surrounded by hay was the old fellow's favourite horse.

> A friend tells us that in every housing office where she's ever worked, people tell this story as having happened to a previous colleague. The only constant appears to be that it's always a

gypsy. It must be the renowned love of animals that suggests the Romanies' inclusion, rather than any form of deep-seated discrimination – surely?

a lousy *night out*

For her hen-night treat, a friend of a friend went with some mates to see one of those raunchy male stripper acts.

The ladies were having a riot ogling the hunky fellas' bulging pecs. They were all getting over-excited, shrieking as the gyrating Adonises disrobed.

Apparently, the bride-to-be got a little tipsy and forced her way to the front of the stage to get a better view. Dancing in a frenzy, she was almost overcome when, at the climax of his act, one of the writhing oiled hunks whipped off his shiny G-string and flung it on to her face.

A couple of days later she was checking her complexion in the bathroom mirror when she noticed a spot near her eyelid. This blemish was a little worrying; with the wedding at the weekend she wanted to look her best for the photographs.

Over the next few days, she tried every kind of cream, but the spot just got larger and larger until she was driven to visit the doctor.

The quack took one look, and informed the girl that he'd have to operate immediately: she had a pubic louse living in her face.

Our publishers told us on no account to mention the Chippendales anywhere near that story, so we won't. Even so, this myth has rapidly done the rounds since the disrobing hunks arrived on the scene – there must be a lot of disgruntled boyfriends eagerly passing it on.

a friend *in need*

A friend of a friend worked in a hospice where there were two elderly bed-ridden men sharing a room.

One old chap had a bed next to a window, and would sit up and describe in loving detail to his friend the children playing in the sunshine, the dogs loping in the park and any particularly nasty street fights.

Every day there were new and amazing scenes, sketched out with such enthusiasm that although he loved the descriptions, the other old chap became sick with jealousy.

Apparently, this went on for some months, until one night the man by the window suddenly groaned loudly and called to his friend, 'Ooh, you've got to ring for help, I don't think I'll last the night . . .'

The other fellow immediately reached for the alarm, but then thought to himself, 'If he goes, I'll get the bed by the window.'

So he lay back and, with the help of a pillow over his ears, ignored his room-mate's death-throe moaning.

In the morning, staff found the poor old bloke stiff as a board, but they reassured his companion that they'd soon have some more company for him.

'I must have the bed next to the window!' snapped the old fellow sharply. The nurses explained it would be easier if he stayed put, but he angrily insisted.

So eventually they lifted him over to the other bed.

Expectantly, he levered himself up and peered out through the window – only to see a solid brick wall.

too cold *to handle*

A friend of a friend who ran a proper old banger lived in the Welsh hills miles from the nearest pub.

Loath though he was to drink and drive, the distance to the nearest hostelry often forced him to negotiate the winding lanes under the influence.

Sadly the local constabulary had often caught him over the limit and recently warned him that one more time would result in a lengthy ban. The prospect of having to walk all that way to the pub really terrified him.

Apparently, one winter's evening, with the snow thick on the ground, he was suffering from a bad cold and gagging for a medicinal snifter.

Driving to the pub without mishap, he settled down in his favourite armchair and, mindful of his licence, took a little more water with his whisky than usual.

Closing time found him still under the limit. Slipping into his car, he reversed gingerly but the bald tyres spun on the ice, and the ancient jalopy slid backwards into the hedge and conked out.

The bloke tried to restart the clapped-out motor but the exhaust pipe was choked up with snow. So he took the old starting handle and waggled one end in the exhaust pipe to unblock it.

As luck would have it, just then a passing copper accosted him, sadly dismissing his remonstrations.

He was convinced that the old fellow was trying to start the car from the wrong end.

a shocking *blunder*

A friend of a friend had been outdoors on his patch preparing for his favourite time of year, blooming spring.

It had rained persistently for days before, so the green-fingered enthusiast ensured he put on his wellington boots before he went out weeding.

After a few hours tugging, he'd done as much as he could handle, wheeled his trusty barrow into the garden shed and walked a little wearily round to the front of the house into the garage, where he'd left his other shoes.

He lifted the up-and-over door, then turned on the light, leaning next to the switch while employing the time-honoured welly-removing technique of putting one foot on the heel of the other boot and pushing.

In his tiredness the bloke was struggling with the trouble-some footwear: wobbling about, tugging on the stuck gum-boot and almost losing his footing.

Apparently, a nosy neighbour, washing his car across the road, spotted the jerking gardener with his hand on the light switch, and put two and two together.

The good Samaritan leapt across the road, picking up a handy baseball bat and aiming to break the hapless gardener's contact with the switch and save him from electrocution.

In a frenzy of misplaced goodwill, he whacked the bat down as hard as possible, breaking his bewildered neighbour's arm in two places.

Another tale that's really going places at the moment, and of which there are two interesting variations: in one the action takes place on an allotment and the injured party leans on a pylon to take his boots off (his father whacks him with a spade to break the contact); and in the other the setting is a kitchen, where a jerking young man is seen holding a wire with his hand on the electric kettle – his wife hits him with a rolling pin to stop the electrocution, but he was only dancing along to the music on his personal stereo.

court *in the act*

A friend of a friend was a magistrate in Newcastle-upon-Tyne, and was once presiding over the case of a German sailor who was charged with being drunk and disorderly.

The unshaven tar was obviously still a little the worse for wear after his overindulgences the night before, and wasn't very coherent when it came to answering even the most basic questions. His limited grasp of English had deserted him, and none of the court officials spoke German, so he was unable to understand anything that was going on.

Recognising that this hardly constituted a fair hearing for the foreign seaman, the magistrate decided to try a different tack. So he asked if anyone in the courtroom was able to speak German.

To his relief, a thin young man in the public gallery with a rockabilly quiff raised his hand, and was ushered to the front.

The makeshift interpreter was positioned next to the defendant, and the magistrate began by asking him to find out the German's name.

Apparently, the young man turned slowly round to the defendant, his faced screwed up with severity, and screamed to the sailor at the top of his voice, 'VOT ISS YOUR NAME!!?'

> The magistrate had no choice but to charge the young man with contempt of court. Actually, that's one of those apocryphal tales that gets passed on in the family as having happened to 'Grandad' or an old uncle. Never proven, never denied, they become part of the family folklore, suitably embellished by each new generation.

hard *to swallow*

A friend of a friend was enjoying the holiday of a lifetime exploring the Amazon rainforest.

She'd been warned about the perilous nature of the local fauna, and not to swim in the river itself no matter how dirty and hot she got.

Apparently the temptation proved too much, and she decided to risk a refreshing naked immersion in the tropical Amazonian water. She was having a wonderful time practising her breaststroke, until her chin dipped under the surface and she swallowed something that made her choke. She was forced to retire to the bank to recover her composure.

After a while back in Britain, the woman found she was

acquiring a voracious appetite for food. Yet her bingeing was having no effect on her waif-like waist.

Soon she was insatiable, tucking into absolutely anything edible. But, incredibly, she was *losing* weight, and her stomach still ached with hunger.

Naturally concerned, she consulted her doctor, who felt her stomach and suggested a prompt visit to a hospital casualty.

They operated at once, and opened up her intestines. There they found a pale, eight-foot anaconda that had grown inside her from the egg she'd inadvertently swallowed.

a fishy *business*

A friend of a friend was throwing a swanky dinner party for her executive husband's new boss and some of the movers and shakers around town.

She had been fretting about what to serve up at such an exclusive gathering. She'd pored through all her glossiest recipe books, and woven together a tantalisingly mouth-watering menu that would have done justice to any of London's top West End restaurants.

The main course was to feature a whole poached salmon. The king of fishes was duly purchased and the next morning the excited hostess got up especially early to lovingly prepare her *pièce de résistance*.

That evening the guests arrived fashionably late, the starter was devoured, the conversation was scintillating and the soirée was going swimmingly.

At a suitable moment, the hostess slipped away from the

table to bring in the salmon from the kitchen. But she breezed through the swing doors to a horrifying sight. Her mangy cat was squatting on the work surface, tucking into the exquisitely spiced fish with great gusto.

She shooed the cat and it fled, leaving the distraught woman in a state of total panic. There was no time to prepare another dish, so she hastily disguised the damage with some judiciously placed cucumber. Then she took it through, holding it aloft to gasps of admiration.

Despite the mishap with the moggy, no one seemed to notice. The meal was acclaimed, and the hostess was complimented on her exceptional culinary skills.

But then popping back into the kitchen to set up the coffee, she noticed all was not well with the cat. In fact, the poor beast was writhing around in convulsions.

She was convinced it must be the salmon that he'd nibbled at earlier. Weighing up the pros and cons of telling the guests they'd just been poisoned, the wretched hostess finally went through and told them what had happened.

Disgusted, they all immediately rushed off to hospital and had their stomachs pumped.

The woman had only just returned home when the doorbell rang. It was the milkman. He'd tried to knock earlier, but couldn't make himself heard above the party noises.

He explained that he was just calling to see if the cat was alright.

Apparently, he'd dropped a milk crate on its head that morning.

A version of this sick cat story was told to us by Richard Madeley, the charming presenter of

13

ITV's justly popular *This Morning* programme, and a keen amateur urban mythologist in his own right. He claims the situation happened to his sister. After hearing that, the invitations to come and eat with Richard's family the next time we're in the area remain firmly on our mantelpieces . . .

However, Richard did know an interesting variation – notably that the groggy cat is discovered after the guests have got home, so the hostess has to ring them all up and suggest the stomach pump.

it's a *lick-up*

A young woman known to a friend in the pub used to live in a spooky old house with her parents in Bath.

When she was sixteen, she was bought a playful puppy which she absolutely adored and which returned her affection twice over. The little spaniel was particularly comforting when her parents stayed away for the night and she was left alone in the rambling, ancient house.

On one such occasion, a nasty windswept night, the teenager played with her puppy before going to sleep, and allowed the dog to sleep on her bed for companionship.

Halfway through the night, she was woken by a tickling sensation on her foot. She clumsily reached under the duvet to push her affectionate puppy away, but he'd already gone.

A little later the same thing happened. Still half asleep, she again shooed the playful mutt away. A few hours passed and the puppy started licking again. But this time after she'd moved her foot away, she became aware of an annoying dripping sound in the bathroom. She wasn't going to get up just to turn a tap off, so she put her head down and didn't wake again until morning.

When she got up, her puppy was nowhere to be seen, but the dripping was still going on, much slower now, so she went straight to the bathroom. To her horror, there in the bathroom was her poor, bloodied puppy, hanging up over the sink with its throat cut. And chillingly daubed on the mirror in canine blood was the legend 'Humans can lick too.'

> Some urban myths are traceable way back into the mists of time but are still referred to currently. In our first book we mentioned the Napoleonic War monkey-hanging incident, when the inhabitants of Hartlepool mistook a monkey caught on an abandoned French vessel for one of Napo-

leon's garlic-breathing sailors, and tried and hanged it as a spy. Despite this myth's antiquity, Hartlepudlians are today still taunted as 'monkey hangers' by other north-easterners, some of whom should remember the maxim concerning people in glass houses, as the next story illustrates.

a barrage *of abuse*

In the early part of the last century before science found a cure to almost every known ill, plagues and diseases were still wreaking havoc with the populace of Britain.

At that time one of the horrors of the day was typhoid. The pernicious disease had gained a toe-hold in the north east of England and was spreading like wildfire.

The good burghers of Wearside were particularly agitated. The disease hadn't reached them yet, and they were determined to keep things that way.

But the Wearsiders' determination clearly outstripped their medical knowledge, and that's how they came to string a large net across the river Wear to arrest the eastward progress of the typhus virus.

blame *backfire*

Back in the heady days before the First World War a society hostess was giving a dinner party for a glittering array of the day's who's who, including Winston Churchill's mother, no less.

The evening was going superbly, each dish cooked to perfection and the staff diligently satisfying every whim without a murmur. Now it was well before the days of nouvelle cuisine and the hearty meal was extremely heavy, with boiled sprouts, cabbage and cauliflower extremely hard to digest politely.

After the dessert, with the conversation as tinkling as a breeze through a chandelier, the hostess felt an irrepressible urge building within her. Oh, the embarrassment! Oh, the shame! But she couldn't fight nature.

Luckily the butler was standing directly behind her chair as a loud rasp trumpeted out. The conversation dried. So to cover her embarrassment the lady of the house blamed the butler.

'Chalfont, stop that at once,' she said.

'Certainly madam,' he retorted. 'Which way did it go?'

man's *best friends*

A menagerie of animal crackers

Poor dumb animals frequently fall foul of the most dangerous animals of them all – humans – and their rancid imaginations. For some reason they bring out the beast in us; on the other hand the whole who's zoo of creation seems intent on biting the hand that feeds it . . .

horse *shoot*

A friend of a friend from Jersey was going rabbit shooting with his mate up in the hills. They planned to check out a place where they'd never shot before that was riddled with rabbit holes, and where you'd often see the furry vermin hopping about their hillside warren.

Most farmers were only too pleased to let the blokes blast their rabbit problem to kingdom come, but the hunters thought it only good manners to ask permission first. They turned up at the farm early one morning and one of them went down to the farmhouse to see the landowner.

The farmer was very hospitable, offering the stranger a steaming mug of strong tea and a hunk of bread and jam. He happily gave the blokes the run of his estate to dispatch as many rabbits as possible. They were a terrible nuisance, forever eating his crops and burrowing under his fences.

Eyeing the gun, the farmer then asked the bloke if he could beg a favour in return.

'There's an old horse up in the top field that's really suffering. I've been meaning to get rid of him, but the knackers want *me* to pay *them* to turn him into dog meat. So perhaps you wouldn't mind shooting him and I'll clear up later,' he said.

Agreeable to shooting anything, the hunter trudged back up the path to his chum. Then a wicked thought occurred to him, and he decided to play a trick on his trigger-happy companion.

They set off together up the hill and when he was out of range of the farmhouse the bloke started swearing about how obnoxious the farmer had been, shouting at him to 'Get off my larnd!' and prodding his rear with a pitch-fork.

Just as they reached the top field, the bloke really laid it on thick. 'That old farmer's really got my goat!' he yelled. 'No one speaks to me like that!' And he lifted his blaster shoulder high and shot the farmer's old horse dead to impress his mate.

But he'd miscalculated his friend's solidarity. Picking up his own shooter, the other bloke yelled, 'Yer, too right,' and promptly slaughtered two cows.

While the above story takes place in the country-side, it illustrates only too well city dwellers' well-supported belief that country folk really hate animals. Urbanites like to believe that the animals on our farmyards all have names like Dobbin, Daisy and Clarabel and live a life of Old Mac-Donald rural bliss. Whereas real country dwellers prefer to see them as new McDonalds and money in the bank. Nowadays Daisy's really called E239875432KZ and she's on more drugs than a Bulgarian weightlifter. Even our indigenous wildlife is under threat from the homicidal yokels. I mean, how many city folk go charging around in a bloodthirsty posse, dressed to kill, with a pack of mad dogs chasing a tiny little terrified adversary – Millwall fans apart?

animal *husbandry*

Treatment of animals in Lancashire varies according to the region. There's a famous incident that happened in West Houghton many moons ago, when an unfortunate cow got its head stuck in a gate.

The best brains in the locality puzzled at how best to save the poor animal without ruining the precious gate. Then some local genius came up with the answer – and sawed the cow's head off. It's an event that's commemorated even today.

In another area of Lancashire (these days Greater Manchester) there's an area called Droylsden, also known as silly country. Animals in Droylsden were traditionally treated with more respect than the women (and perhaps still are). On one celebrated occasion, during a festival of some sort, a brass band was marching in a parade, and some of the simple locals were so excited that they put their pig on a wall to afford it a better view. These days a pub stands on that very site and (surprise surprise) it's called 'The Pig On The Wall' – there's immortality for you.

thereby *hangs a tail*

A solicitor from Berkshire liked nothing better than a good hard ride first thing Sunday morning, and generally on his horse, an old, grey-whiskered stallion who'd been a bit of a tyrant in his day. Now, in his broad-beamed maturity, the most dangerous thing about the horse was his breath.

One lovely summer's morning nature was in her glory. Perfumed wild flowers banked high along the verge, birds chattered and the sun shone, and the brief was at peace with the world as his old mount clip-clopped beneath him. But a few minutes along the lane, the idyllic scene was shattered by the ominous high-pitched barking of an approaching dog. Immediately, the spooked old nag stiffened, fretting and huffing as its rider grew concerned that he might bolt or rear up as had happened before.

The cur came barrelling down the road with the sort of irritating repetitive baying only an overexcited Jack Russell can produce, and the horse continued to lurch and froth nervously while the rider had to use all his best dressage techniques to maintain control.

Just as things seemed to be going awry, the solicitor noticed an old white gate half hidden amongst some bushes, and had an idea. He reached inside the pocket of his tweed hacking jacket and found to his delight some hairy string.

Patting dobbin to calm him down, he carefully dismounted and lurching forward to grab the canine, smoothly looped one end of the twine round its collar and the other by a testy reef-knot to the old gate. Then he remounted and resumed the gentle clip-clop down the lane away from the pesky pooch.

Apparently, just at that moment, an InterCity train hurtled past by the side of the lane. Horrified, the solicitor turned round to see his worst fears confirmed: seconds after the train had passed, the white gate creaked up high in the air – with the little Jack Russell still attached, hanging the poor mutt.

messy *moggy*

A haulage firm based near King's Lynn used to allow a number of feral cats on site in order to keep the problem of vermin under control. But casualties were frequent; the cats would take shelter anywhere around the artics – on the wheels, on the axles, under the cab – and never seemed to learn. So the company sealed an arrangement with a local vet so that any cat injured could be taken, any time, day or night, to the surgery for treatment.

The scheme proved successful, and in return for a number of recuperating felines, the boss of the company would drop round the odd treat off the back of one of his lorries.

Then one morning the haulage guv'nor got a furious call from the vet. Ear still burning, he called his drivers in to explain. After a minute one stepped forward.

'Well, boss,' he said, 'I ran over a cat in me lorry, right, and I went down the vet's. But it was closed, so I slipped the cat under the door with a note.'

An American version of these 'stupid things to do with a dead cat'-type stories has a couple renting a house in a neighbourhood, then going on a touring holiday for three weeks. After a few days they notice a dead cat in the back of their car – they've got a sun-roof and reckon it must've fallen in from a tree-branch. They recognise the cat as their neighbours', and keep it in a bag. At the end of their holiday, they return home to find the neighbours are now on holiday, so they thoughtfully deposit the moggy in its owners' postbox and keep schtum.

absolutely *charming*

A consignment of wicker baskets arrived fresh from India for a well-known 'lifestyle' department store. They were the classic 'snake-charmer' type, which had been selling like hot cakes to people who loved the genuine 'ethnic' look.

But this particular batch was even more realistic – one potential customer lifted the lid of the last one in the shop, let out a terrified shriek and collapsed in a faint.

Coiled up in the bottom of the basket was a deadly poisonous black mamba, snoozing peacefully.

otter *rubbish*

According to a publican friend of my parents, in the Dartmoor area of Devon – prime 'grockle' territory – animal lovers were so concerned at the depletion of local freshwater otters that they recently took to equipping the ones they could find with a harness and a bulky waterproof radio transmitter pack on their backs, so wildlife experts could keep tabs on them.

But the landlord was sceptical about how much use they would be, and one night one of his regulars, a man renowned for his hatred of summer visitors, burst in looking befuddled and demanding a medicinal double brandy.

'What's up, John?' asked the concerned barman.

'Those bloody tourists must really be getting to me now,'

said the flustered bloke. 'I've just seen an otter wearing a rucksack.'

hook, *line and shooter*

A friend's grandad who had fallen on hard times, but was a keen huntin', shootin' 'n' fishin' countryman, took to poaching to supplement his meagre pension.

Apparently the old goat saw himself as some kind of latter-day Robin Hood, taking from the rich and giving to the poor, i.e. himself. He loved a well-hung pheasant, fresh game and river fish, finding out, as a lot of people do, that things always taste better if you don't pay for them. (Just ask the royal family.)

One day, he found himself at an idyllic private lake set in the woods of a large country estate. It was one of his regular uninvited haunts and terrorised by a notorious monster pike called 'Old Larry' – an adversary of the old man's from way back.

The old poacher had had little luck with his shotgun that morning, and laying the shooter down on a nearby rock settled down to try his luck with a rod and line. But he hadn't had so much as a nibble in hours and was about to give it up as a bad day all round when he felt his line bang like it was stuck on a train. He'd hooked Old Larry.

After a titanic battle to land him, the old man was chuffed to have dispatched his old foe but was nevertheless disappointed that the pike wouldn't make good eating. So tossing the monster fish to one side, he cast out his line again.

Old Larry wasn't finished, though.

In a fit of thrashing the monster pike managed to get his huge tail caught in the blaster's trigger – shooting the poor old poacher dead.

> There's a remarkably similar tale doing the rounds which has as its preferred victim a member of the upper classes. The toff in question casually throws a brace of recently dispatched grouse (or *grice*) into the back of his 4×4 station wagon on the glorious twelfth. But one game bird, with its dying breath, hooks a claw into a shotgun trigger and blows the hunter's legs clean off. Honestly, who would believe that?

owners *and their dogs*

A friend who spent some time working abroad knew of a Swedish acquaintance who owned a lovely lustrous-coated Red Setter dog that he had had for years. This Scandinavian bachelor enjoyed nothing better than to rove the verdant pastures of his homeland with his faithful friend by his side – and the same went for his dog.

One day, however, the dog was limping around bow-legged and looking very sorry for itself. The bloke took his poor pet to the vet, who set about examining between its legs, where the problem seemed to lie.

A few minutes later the vet broke off – he'd found a sheep tick burrowing into the dog's leg, and removed it. That was obviously the source of the dog's discomfiture, but he'd discovered something else in his examination. 'It

27

doesn't mean anything really,' he smiled, 'but did you know your dog only has one testicle?'

'No, I didn't,' the owner laughed, and patted his dog.

But the revelation set his mind in motion, and the next time he went to the bathroom at home, the bachelor spent a moment giving himself a quick once-over in the wedding tackle area. And in an odd twist of the old adage about dogs looking like their owners, to his amazement the bloke discovered he too only had one ball.

> So when this Swedish gentleman used the common compliment that something was 'the dog's bollocks', somehow it didn't carry the same weight.

left *in the lurch*

Before the hideously violent breeds of dog like the Rottweiler and Pit Bull, before even the Dobermann pinscher, the status symbol on urban council estates was a lurcher – the mother of all maniacal mutts.

The lurcher was a lean, wild-looking beast, and for some reason you could only get a decent one from a gypsy.

A friend remembers someone at school in Deptford whose father set his heart on one of these vicious animals, and was told by someone in his pub that there was one for sale from some travellers on their encampment out of town. So he promptly went in pursuit of the puppy, and fixed a deal with the owner.

The powerful tawny beast grew quickly and looked great with its studded collar on, terrorising the streets and snarling at passers-by. But as the lurcher began to grow, the family noticed that it just growled, never barked, and had a long tail with a tuft on the end which it would never, ever wag.

Eventually, the owner thought that the reason it wouldn't wag its tail was down to its state of mind, so he went to the vet to ask why it was unhappy.

To his surprise, the animal doctor immediately explained why it wouldn't wag its tail . . . it was a lion cub.

> The infamous gypsy lurcher, for those who don't know, is defined in the dictionary as a breed of dog that's a cross between a greyhound and a collie, often used by poachers for retrieving game. The expensive ones would have the brain of the collie and the speed of the greyhound; the less fortunate ones (vice-versa) went even faster straight to the bottom of the canal tied to a pile of bricks. One last thing: it's said the greyhound's legendary viciousness is due to its brain being too big for its tiny skull. John Selwyn Gummer? Say no more . . .

stair *crazy*

My uncle knows a bandsaw pattern cutter down the umbrella factory whose dog is in urgent need of an animal psychologist.

The bloke lives alone in a pokey old red-brick terraced house that has only recently been able to boast an inside toilet. It hasn't been decorated in living memory and reeks of burnt cooking fat.

Feeling a bit lonely, the bachelor decided to buy a puppy for company, and rescued a cute black and brown Manchester terrier (or mongrel) from the pet shop window sawdust. At first everything went swimmingly. The playful mutt was a real joy, forever bounding around, getting into scrapes and always, always wagging its whiplash tail. The most satisfying thing was how easy it was to train. Fetching sticks, playing dead, getting the paper – nothing seemed too tricky for it to master.

Apparently, one breathy morning the bloke was blearily shuffling barefooted along the threadbare landing carpet in his rancid pyjama trousers, heading to the bathroom for a shave. He'd reached the top of the stairs when he trod in something soft, warm and pungent. He furiously sought out the skulking hound, dragged him to the stairs and rubbed his nose in it, hard, before flinging the howling mutt down the stairs.

'That's taught him a lesson he won't forget,' the bloke mused to himself as he limped, toes-up, to the bathroom.

And how right he was. The dog knew that if he crapped on the top step, he'd get thrown down the stairs.

And he enjoyed it so much, he did it every morning from that day forward.

the grate *escape*

At a friend's wedding in darkest Wales, an Australian sheep farmer was telling how in the early seventies a number of his sheep discovered a method whereby they could defeat the cattle grids placed in the roads to prevent them from straying.

As every schoolkid knows, the grids are a series of heavy-duty steel bars placed over a deep trench in the road surface. The sheep are unable to walk across because their hooves are too small and they'd slip between the bars, but trucks can easily drive over.

Seemingly the old adage 'the grass is always greener' applies for sheep too, and this flock had come to know that the best way to overcome the man-made obstruction and reach fresh grazing pasture was to curl up in a ball, hedgehog-like, and roll over the grid's bars.

An old hill farmer, who'd overheard the Aussie shepherd relate the tale, quizzed him further, asking when this peculiar modification in sheep behaviour had occurred.

'About 1975,' replied the man from down under.

'That's queer,' ruminated the ancient Welshman, who'd been close to sheep all his life. 'The same thing started here about two years later; I wonder how they passed it on?'

Sheep are renowned for their stupidity, but how much do we really know about animals? They say that dolphins are incredibly intelligent, but it's often asked, 'If they're so smart how come there are no dolphins in Mensa?' We think the answer is clear − dolphins never go to work, but enjoy a life of leisure splashing about all day in the tropical sea, eating and drinking as much as they want. So who's stupid? Our clever aquatic mammalian chums are also said to have their own lingo, communicating ideas with a language of squeaks and crackles which is obviously more intelligent than most radio DJs.

Rats are also thought to have more than a

modicum of brain power, and the Chunnel poses a new problem apart from the original fear that foreign rabies-carrying vermin would come flooding through and biting every baby in Kent. Apparently the reverse is true. Rats are at present emigrating to the continent in hordes, leading to such a Euro-rat problem that ferrets from all over England have been stolen to cope. You know what they say about a sinking ship . . .

ruff guide *to Spain*

One of my gran's old pals from chorus-line music-hall days was on holiday with a bunch of senior citizens in Benidorm.

The old dear loved animals, and every morning she would take a few scraps out to the compound gates and feed the local strays on the beach. There were scrawny Spanish pooches of all shapes, all typically tiny, and being a soft-hearted old girl, she immediately fell for the skinniest little wretch of the bunch, and cossetted it most of all.

When the holiday drew to a close the old dear couldn't bear to leave her scruffy little chum to the hard life of the streets, and ignoring the stringent quarantine regulations and the danger of rabies, she resolved to smuggle the toy dog back to Blighty.

With the diversionary tactics of a few of the other senior citizens, involving a dodgy pacemaker and some Winter-green's ointment, she breezed through customs and got her little pal home in a jiffy. Letting her new pet out of his parcel, the old lady introduced him to her cat.

The tom took one look and attacked. A terrible fight ensued. Plants went flying, curtains were ruined and an umbrella stand spilled over.

The old dear finally broke them up and there was blood everywhere. She rushed the poor little Spanish dog straight to the vet's. The animal doctor took one look and asked her what she thought it was.

'What can you mean? It's a dog,' said the elderly dame.

'I've got news for you,' said the vet sternly. 'This, madam, is a giant gutter rat.'

The kind-hearted lady and her cherished rat-dog formed the title story of Jan Harold Brunvand's collection of American apocryphal stories *The Mexican Pet*, and is one of those that appears rooted in the observation of the sorry condition

of some Spanish/Mexican breeds, and the misplaced sympathy of those who ignore the threat
of rabies. Who'd be a chihuahua, though? The
diminutive dogs are all too often the butt of
mythical accidents: frequently sat upon and killed
or attacked by big domestic cats who think they
are rats.

cat *in the bag*

Driving home from work one day, a friend of my aunt's
who lives in a less than salubrious area ran over her pet cat.

She was very upset at the moggy's demise, but being a
practical woman immediately set about clearing up the
unfortunate animal in preparation for a decent burial. So
she popped the squashed beast into a handy green Marks
and Spencer's bag, then opened the boot to get her
shopping.

Just as she battled with too much shopping, a scruffy
woman rushed up and snatched the M&S bag with the
dead cat in it and scarpered around the corner.

Seconds later, there was a squeal of brakes and a sickening
thud. Aunt's friend dropped her shopping and dashed to
see what had happened. There lying crumpled on the
ground surrounded by a group of people was the bag-
snatcher.

An ambulance was called and the woman stretchered
inside. The paramedics were just closing the rear door
when someone piped up, 'Here, don't forget this – she was
looking at that when she got hit.'

And he popped the M&S bag inside the ambulance.

purr-*silly*

A woman on the new estate just up the road from us had recently moved into a brand spanking new dream home with her two nippers and hubby in tow.

The kids loved the new house but wanted a pet, so she bought a kitten and took it home for the kids. Everything was going swimmingly until one day Tiddles disappeared. The distraught family looked everywhere: under the bed, in the airing cupboard – all the usual places – but the miniature moggy was nowhere to be seen.

With the kids in tears in the kitchen the washing machine stopped and a faint whimpering was heard. Inside, they found a bedraggled pussy, mewing but none the worse for wear, even though he'd been through the whole cycle, including the spin.

> The next story follows a similar plot to the tale of the unfortunate budgerigar in our previous book, *Urban Myths*, but it's such a neat variation we thought it deserved an airing.

feather *light*

It was those hazy crazy lazy days of summer again, and a mate was looking after his nan's budgerigar while she kept her Wednesday afternoon appointment at the hairdresser's for a shampoo and set.

The little feathered chap was looking a bit down in the beak, so the lad let it out of its cage to stretch its wings.

Like a blue thunderbolt the grass parakeet shot out of

his hand and smashed straight into the window. Clearly quite dazed and confused, the ruffled fancy bird was limping forlornly in circles on the kitchen lino.

Its leg was obviously very painful, and possibly broken. Reckoning a little first aid was in order, the resourceful lad took some cotton and tied a matchstick to the injured budgie's limb to act as a splint, before popping him back behind bars. The peg-leg hopped across the bottom of his cage towards his cuttlefish. Then, inevitably, the match ignited on the sandpaper sheet, the flames spreading quickly to his feathers and barbecuing the poor bird.

gecko *blaster*

A bespectacled young man who used to frequent a friend's cafe was keen on exotic wildlife and kept a gecko in his run-down flat which he would stare at for hours on end. The tropical house-lizard was afforded a parsimonious diet by its owner, who thought that the effort of obtaining live locusts – the gecko's staple – was enough trouble already.

But the gecko soon tired of its diet, and, as a kind of hunger strike, began eating only one or two of the live insects and letting the others skip around its tank without batting an eyelid. Inevitably, one day the young fellow came home to find his treasured gecko dead.

Some weeks later, on a balmy summer's morning, the bloke was awoken by an odd rustling noise in the living room, but when he investigated, he could only trace it to the wall, so it was obviously next door's problem.

A week later, the rustling had intensified into a scratching along the whole of one wall which was driving him to distraction, and the bloke decided it was time for action. So he took a hammer and chisel to the plaster and smashed a huge hole in the living room wall. But as the plaster fell away, he was shocked to see that the entire cavity was filled with locusts – obviously escaped from his gecko's tank – and they swarmed all over him, nibbling his cardigan, before swooping through the open window and massing over his neighbours' back gardens, devouring every sunflower, lettuce and lawn in the locality.

airmail *special*

A friend remembers a lad at his West Country school who for some time kept up correspondence with a pen-pal in Nigeria. It wasn't quite the same as exchanging letters with a Texan kid (they always go on about how big things are – 'mice the size of houses', that sort of thing), but came close.

You see, they developed a rivalry about their respective homelands to such an extent that their descriptions bore little resemblance to the reality of life in mundane Poole, Dorset or Ibadan, southern Nigeria.

The British lad was sick of all the wild animals his African correspondent would brag about encountering, and his Nigerian counterpart was fed up with all the snide comments about how civilised England was and how much better the police were.

They went on for months trying to outdo each other. Eventually the Nigerian boy wrote about a snake he kept as a pet. He said it was the most poisonous snake in the world, and could kill within seconds of a bite.

The English lad, by now scornful of the other's bragging, wrote back mocking him, saying he'd looked it up in his *World of Wonder* book, and there weren't any very poisonous snakes in that part of Africa.

A few weeks later, he was surprised to receive a package with a Nigerian postmark. Inside, to his horror, was a poisonous snake, luckily quite dead and past its mongoose-sparring days. A note fell out of the parcel.

Oddly, it seemed the spiteful package was not from his pen-pal.

The note said, 'I've been reading your impertinent letters

to our young man here in Ibadan, and let me tell you we in the office are very angry at your attitude, so we sent you some proof that poisonous snakes do exist in his district!'

And it was signed by the chief postmaster in his pen-pal's locality.

cheap *day rover*

A story recently appeared in a local free sheet in London's East End concerning a dog that had followed behind his owner (on his way to work and oblivious to his pet's presence) as far as Mile End tube station.

As if that wasn't bad enough, the dog then ran along the tracks after the tube train his owner was on, eventually surfacing at Stratford, one stop away along the Central Line.

Luckily he'd suffered only slight injuries.

> Believable? Just enough for the story writer to follow up the exclusive and phone London Underground for details. Their spokesman hadn't heard of that particular incident, but wasn't surprised at the tale. Some time ago, he said, a dog spotted on the tracks at King's Cross had disappeared down a tunnel only to reappear some time later at Earl's Court on the other side of London (11 stops if the dog used the most direct route, the Piccadilly Line), apparently managing to avoid the frequent trains, and evidently none the worse for the journey (unlike most London Underground users).

This is clearly an urban myth in an early stage of evolution. Watch its development with interest.

The next tale also proves the seductive power of urban myths. The yarn even fooled cynical, hard-bitten TV news journalists.

brushed *off*

A local news team got wind of a peculiar story that at a rustic pub deep in the Kent countryside local farmers were organising fox-hunting posses.

Nothing unusual in that, you might think, but these were posses with a difference. No traditional trappings of horse and hound, red jackets and stirrup cups – this lot were tooled up with pump-action shotguns and riding souped-up Range Rovers. It wasn't the unspeakable in pursuit of the uneatable, more like a case of Rambo versus Reynard – all-out war with the native Basil Brushes.

The news team blazed a trail to the reported scene of carnage, lubricating a local witness who claimed to have seen it all.

A friend of his who lived in a small cottage down a dark winding lane said he'd been woken at midnight by the rumblings of a large pantechnicon and had drawn back the curtains to see the huge truck drop its tailgate. As it did, dozens of foxes flooded out barking and bounding over each other on their way to freedom. Clearly stencilled on the side of the lorry was the inscription 'Lambeth Council Works'.

Apparently, the foxes had become such an urban nuisance that the council's dog catchers had been charged with bringing the vermin under control. But they hadn't the heart to put them down, and instead shipped them out to a better life in the sticks. And as city foxes are far tougher than their country cousins, the informant continued, the rural gentry had set up the extermination brigades. Impressed, the news team scented blood and called the RSPCA for comment.

The officer answered, 'I'm sorry, but I think you've been barking up the wrong tree. We've heard this all before; last year it was in mid-Wales, and the year before that in the Peak District.'

am-*brushed*

Up in the Trossachs a well-to-do couple lived in a comfortable 1930s semi on the edge of town. They were animal lovers, and especially fond of their daffy cat.

The tabby was quite a character and had been down to the vet's so often that the staff all knew him by name and looked forward to his regular visits. Run over twice, leaping off the roof at a sparrow and swallowing a ball of string – the couple were getting concerned that the accident-prone moggy was overdrawn on his account as far as lives were concerned.

But his dicing with death didn't seem to curb the mad moggie's behaviour. One day when he was climbing the bathroom curtains as usual, he lost his footing and plummeted, backside first, on to the upended toilet brush. The owners heard a startled yowl and rushed upstairs to find the poor animal with the lavatory brush jammed up its fundamental as far as the handle. The worried owners raced

41

down to the vet's. The animal doctor couldn't believe his eyes.

'I know cats like to keep themselves scrupulously clean,' he muttered, getting a good grip on the bogbrush handle, 'but this is ridiculous.'

mythellaneous

Nature

* Pigs are very good swimmers, but they daren't take the plunge for fear of their razor-sharp, thrashing trotters slitting their throats

* Robins have regional accents that they pick up from their relatives and friends

* Starlings can impersonate car alarms and switch them off

* One scene in the Bayeux Tapestry (1067) depicts a kangaroo (Australia was 'discovered' 700 years later). It's somewhere near panel 48

* Cuddly koala bears are actually vicious – one once bit the Queen

* When a tiger's skin splits along its back, that beast will become a man-eater

* Sri Lankan elephant boys give their charges 'speed' to make them work just that little bit faster

* If a large vicious dog attacks you, the best way to avoid being savaged is to grab its front legs and swiftly yank them apart sideways, killing it instantly

* If a cow licks your bald pate, your hair grows back – but it has to be the right type of cow

* You can save a Spanish bull from certain death in the ring only by marrying it

* New Age travellers get stoned by licking a certain type of toad
* If you pick a hamster up by the tail, its eyes pop out
* A woman once lost her watch on a Devon beach. Years later, her husband caught a fish in the same spot and it had her watch inside – still keeping perfect time

mean *machines*

Spanners in the works

Driving draws out the demon within. Everyone changes when they sit behind a wheel, but this collection of car capers is souped up beyond belief. If you're already heading for a breakdown, these stories'll have you running out for a pony and trap.

a low *note*

One of our old dinner ladies from school was chattering on the corner of a heavily parked-up busy road when she saw a flaky driver, veering from side to side, prang a stationary motor.

Expecting the driver to carry on regardless, as so many people seem to do in this day and age, she and others in the street were pleasantly surprised to see the considerate driver stop, earnestly examine the damage and take a pen and paper from his car and write down the details. He then placed the note under the damaged car's windscreen wiper before driving on.

A minute later, the owner of the damaged car appeared. He was distressed to see his dented wing but pleased to see the note, which he read carefully.

Then he exploded. The passer-by said she'd witnessed the accident and asked what the matter was: didn't he have the other driver's details on the note?

'See for yourself,' muttered the angry owner, showing her the paper, which read:

'I've just crunched your car, and because there are loads of nosy people watching me, I'm pretending to write down my name, registration number and insurance details.'

on *the skids*

The younger brother of a friend at college in Newcastle-upon-Tyne paid his elder sibling a visit a few years ago, and being a bit boracic, elected not to travel by pricey train, but one of those new-style, non-stop luxury coaches, the 'Rapide'.

He caught the double-decker for the five-hour journey north and took his place upstairs in one of the video seats next to a nun reading her Bible, and settled down to watch the film, *Straw Dogs*.

Halfway up the M1, after some refreshments and a short nap, the young man wasn't alone in hearing the call of nature from his bowels, and tottered down the aisle to the toilet in the centre of the coach.

But midway through his exertions, the coach had to suddenly swerve to avoid a serious accident and slammed on the anchors.

The young fellow at his toilet was caught unawares, and was violently thrown off the bog seat against the slim door. Unfortunately for him, it wasn't securely locked and also opened *out*wards.

He was hurled out into the aisle, skidding along on his bottom with his trousers and underpants around his ankles, coming to a halt under the startled gaze of the nun and other gawping passengers.

motorway *microwave*

A woman who works in the same biscuit factory as my dad's sister was driving out of a motorway service station one muggy afternoon, when she spotted an abandoned microwave by the hard shoulder.

Thinking it had probably fallen off the back of a lorry and that it was just the sort of thing her handyman husband would love to get working, the woman pulled over. She lifted it carefully on to her back seat, then continued on her way.

Some minutes later, a police car came screaming up behind her, flashing her to pull over. They looked in her car and asked her what she thought she was doing with that in the back. Slightly rattled, she hurriedly explained her story.

'There's one small problem,' said the smirking officer. 'That's not a microwave, madam, it's one of our speedcheck boxes.'

> The new automatic camera speedchecks, which take snapshots of speeding motorists' number plates and automatically dispatch a fine to them, have already created widespread indignation, spawning the inevitable apocryphal stories. Apparently the insidious new tool of the Big Brother state was invented and developed by a Dutch racing driver. Thanks, mate.

tow *job*

One of the first places to have the automatic speedchecks fitted was near Wembley on London's north circular road.

Recently a motorist known to a friend was quite taken aback to receive a docket from the Met advising him that following the examination of photographic evidence, he was being fined for exceeding the speed limit.

The thing was, his car had broken down on the morning of the date stated, so he demanded to see the pictures for himself.

Down at the station, he was shown the prints, which indeed showed his car crossing a junction at considerable speed and with the light on red.

But, as the driver pointed out, the photo missed out a crucial point – he was being towed by a breakdown truck at the time.

getting *the boot*

In 1976 an aspiring young property speculator from Liverpool arrived at the conclusion that if he was going to cash in on his wealth by having success with the fairer sex, he needed a smart motor. The dream car the scouser set his heart on was a Jensen Interceptor – the ultimate crumpet-puller. The problem was he wasn't particularly flush yet – cash flow, you understand, he hadn't realised any of his assets – so he had to go for the cheapest around.

As luck would have it, he saw a nearly-new metallic bronze Interceptor in a local showroom dirt cheap. Suspecting it was a square-wheel job, or at least a Friday car, he nevertheless checked it out and was well impressed.

When asked about previous owners, the salesman looked a little shifty; still, it drove like a dream, had a full MOT, tax and warranty, and smelt like a high-class hooker's bathroom – best of all it was a bargain.

He bought it. But after a week, in the big heat of '76, the pleasant perfume faded, replaced by a worrying whiff. It was an unusually strong musty odour that just wouldn't go no matter which proprietary cleaning fluids or perfumes he applied.

He tried the lot – Magic Tree, Feu Orange and even

the ultimate deterrent, a hockey player's jock deodorant –
but the nasty niff just wouldn't budge.

Moreover it proved a right turn-off with the ladies,
which really rankled with him.

So a month after purchase he was back complaining
about this obstinate odour. To his surprise and delight, the
salesman swiftly accepted the fault and refunded his money
in full, no questions asked.

Suspicious, the scouser asked what the real story was
with this car.

The salesman came clean: the car had previously been
in the possession of a shady local businessman. When he'd
gone on a planned trip to Turkey and months later hadn't
returned, his car had been reclaimed from the airport.

The police checked it over thoroughly and eventually
found the businessman's badly decomposed body in the
boot.

It's that time again – hitchhiker scare stories? We
got 'em!

hitched *up*

Two New Age travellers went to Bristol to look at an old
ambulance advertised in the paper. It was no good, and
they decided to hitch back to the south Devon moor
where they lived.

They were so rank looking that they were standing on
the bend of the road for hours without any driver so much
as looking at them.

Then a late model hatchback slowed down in front of

them, and they swiftly took up the offer, jumping in – one in the back next to a pile of Sainsbury's bags, the other in the front passenger seat. The woman driver stiffly asked them where they wanted to go. They explained where they lived, but said they'd settle for halfway as it was such a long distance.

As it was, the driver seemed eager to please them and drove them all the way to Haldon Moor, but without saying a word – they assumed she'd just passed her test and didn't want any distractions, so they just gave her appropriate directions.

An hour later, they arrived at the travellers' destination. The woman looked visibly relieved when they got out and thanked them for 'not attacking her'. The two lads looked puzzled, and thanked her profusely for the lift. 'Lift?' said the woman. 'But I thought you were hijacking me!'

A classic misapprehension, given extra potency for the inclusion of that modern West Country pariah, the New Age traveller. Untrustworthy hitchhikers invading the security of our private motors crop up again and again, some simply to vanish into ghostly thin air, others with more insidious or violent intent, as follows.

eye *eye*

In the early eighties, some time before the 'first crusade' in Britain by Billy Graham, a friend of a friend was driving alone one night through the rain-swept suburbs of south London.

51

He saw a wretched-looking hitchhiker by the side of the road, and taking pity on him, stopped to give him a lift. But as soon as the hiker got in, the kindly driver began to regret it.

As they pulled away, the scrawny passenger stared at him with crazed eyes, deeply unsettling the driver, who asked hurriedly, 'Where are you heading?'

But the passenger ignored him and persisted with his disturbing gaze.

After a few minutes, the driver could stand it no longer.

'Look,' he said, pulling over and turning to face the hitchhiker, 'why are you staring at me like that?'

'I was sent by Jesus – to stop you,' the hitchhiker shouted.

Then he quickly whipped out a knife and stabbed it into the driver's eye, before opening the car door and scampering off into the night.

cow *down below!*

A fax salesman who's forever pestering us on the phone was tooling up the A1 one gorgeous sunny day in his ace new cerise Mazda convertible.

He was having a magic time: shades on, Springsteen blasting out, rag-top down, catching some rays.

Then out of the blue a huge black and white Friesian cow landed in the back seat with a bone-crunching thud.

He careered over to the hard shoulder and tried to remove the poor dead beast, but it was unbelievably heavy and stuck fast. So he drove off the main road to the nearest village and found the local garage.

Once they'd stopped laughing, the grease monkeys

managed to lift the cow out with an engine hoist, but the car was covered in unspeakable muck.

Before he could face the rest of the journey, the driver nipped into the local pub for a stiffener.

Inside, he got talking to the publican and related his story.

As he did, another drinker piped up. 'You must have been below me,' he laughed. 'I just ploughed my lorry into a herd of cows on the bridge over the A1.'

the driver's *seat*

Over on the worse side of the Pennines in Yorkshire, there's a stretch of the M62 heading towards Leeds that's brilliant for racing down.

But as you might expect the spoilsport police frown upon this fun and hide out behind shrubbery and such-like in their jam-butties, praying for a speeding motorist – especially if it's a smart-arse lawyer – to intimidate.

One such cheerless M-way cop and his sidekick often patrolled that stretch. His idea of a brilliant laugh was to look out for his wife in her car coming home after work, then blast up her rear lit up like a Christmas tree, lights and siren a-blazing. They'd pull over and have a chat and a snog on the hard shoulder before she continued on her way.

Evidently this happened practically every week, until one evening the officer's wife was running one of her athletic badminton chums to the sports centre down the M62. Ramming her foot down when she came to the hill, she was soon accompanied by the wailing siren, and pulled over.

To impress her friend, instead of getting out of the car, she slipped down her undergarments and pressed her ample bottom against the window. Unbeknown to her, her husband was on duty elsewhere and his replacement – also his chief – was apparently far from impressed.

whiplash *effect*

The decade that taste forgot, the seventies, sprouted many a cock-eyed fashion trend – 28-inch loons, sky-high plat-forms, hot pants, tank tops, boob tubes and the rest.

Even cars weren't immune to the attentions of the style gurus, and no boy racer would be seen dead without fat rubber, flared arches, jacked rear axle, leopardskin seat covers, CB, wild paint job and go-faster stripes – it was the custom.

One mate had the lot and more. His red and white Starsky-and-Hutch Cortina sported not just the standard huge back wheels and illuminated rear axle, but also a green sunstrip visor with 'Daz' on one side and 'Sit Vac' on the other.

His mates used to hang around the bus stop with bags of chips, squealing 'Rubber!!' and drooling as the flash Cortina burned rubber, wheel-spinning, sliding and swerving. They all thought the car was 'it' – no way could Daz improve the beast.

But he did. One afternoon he bought the ultimate in cool accessories, a 10ft fibreglass whiplash aerial.

That night he couldn't wait to show off to his mates, and left a trail of flame behind him burning down to the bus stop flat out. All the kids were there, crowded on the edge of the pavement. The Cortina came tooling up right at them, and screeched to a halt.

The urchins stared agog at the swirling monster aerial. Then it viciously whipped forward, brutally slicing into one lad's skull, killing him stone dead.

slip *road*

A friend of a friend travels the country in women's underwear . . . Actually that's not strictly true – he's every dentist's dream and every paying mother's nightmare, a sales rep for a sweet company.

His crucial work takes him the length and breadth of

the M6 tempting the papershops of the Midlands and North with his sherbet dip and midget gems.

In the course of plying his sticky trade he came across a curious phenomenon. On the northbound carriageway of the M6 motorway, just near his home town of Preston, there's a badly signposted slip road for works traffic only, which loops steeply down under the motorway.

Apparently, there was a cock-up in the drawing office during construction, and the resultant road scheme creates a Möbius strip effect, as the travelling salesman discovered.

The tired rep was thrashing his way back to Preston through the driving rain one night, and found himself on the troublesome turn-off by mistake.

He followed the sharp curve round, only to find himself moments later careering the wrong way up the southbound fast lane of the M6.

> Makes a change to blame the authorities for a motorist going the wrong way up a motorway – in most apocryphal stories, it's a senile old man or woman who drives their old banger for miles in the wrong lane before being stopped by the traffic cops.

a nasty *set-to*

When my uncle left the Paras, one of his mates got a job for a building company driving a huge cement mixer truck.

Driving the diesel-guzzling concrete monster thrilled him to bits, but working on big ready-mix jobs often kept him away from home for days at a time. And although

he loved his young wife dearly, he became convinced she
was having an affair. It was the little things: she'd started
wearing skimpy tops and too much perfume.

Apparently, in an effort to catch her out, he drove home
early one day. Sure enough, there was a flash red soft-top
sports car parked outside the house, and the upstairs curtains
were closed.

Wiping a tear from his eye with his fist, he backed up
his truck, and filled the convertible to the brim with quick
setting cement.

Job done, he trundled round the corner to see what
would happen. He'd just hauled on the handbrake when a
skinny bloke nipped out of the house, hopped on his hidden
bike and wobbled off down the road.

An alternative, slightly less misogynist ending to

the above yarn has the wife in tears because the hubby's mistaken jealousy has ruined the brand-new car she'd bought him as a surprise present. Apparently she had been secretly working as a barmaid in the evenings to afford the treat and bought the car from her earnings. The man she is in the house with turns out to be the salesman who has just delivered the motor.

caught *in the headlights*

A friend of my uncle is a retired carpenter who lives up on the edge of the Pennines.

He drove a lovely old polished Rover of an evening and regularly toured up to his local in the hills where they don't know the meaning of closing time. The bloke didn't overindulge, and usually left just before eleven.

But practically every night as he drove back along an unlit and particularly winding stretch of road two grebos on monster bikes spitting horsepower would really put the willies up him.

The huge greasers, headlights blazing, would take up the whole road, coming the opposite way. They blazed towards him with no thought for road safety, playing chicken and forcing him to swerve off the road into hedges to avoid crashing.

This situation went on for some time. Then one night, the bloke was driving back with a little more Dutch courage than usual coursing through his veins.

He spotted the bikers a few bends ahead.

Slamming his foot down, he hammered along the switch-back road thinking this time he'd show them who's boss.

He rounded the last corner into the glare of the bikers' two headlights and thundered for the gap between them – too late realising the headlights actually belonged to an articulated lorry.

> There's a distinct similarity there to another 'worm turning' bikers story, in which a driver in a motorway cafe is harassed by a chapter of Hell's Angels while eating his dinner. They stub their fags out in his fried egg and generally humiliate him, but he doesn't retaliate, just walks slowly out. 'Not much of a man, was he?' sneers one of the bikers. 'Not much of a driver, either,' observes the waitress. 'He's just driven his truck over a row of motorbikes.'

a lot *of bollards*

A friend's normally teetotal old ballroom dancing teacher was dragged into celebrating south Molesey Over-sixties paso-doble pairs' victory over Chalfont St Giles district in the southern area final.

After just a couple of sweet sherries the deft hoofer really got the taste, and began putting them away like there was no tomorrow. Unfortunately there was a tomorrow – and a journey home first. It wasn't until well after time that he hazily remembered he'd come in his car. As he lived some way round the M25 there was no other way back – a taxi was out as he'd blown his wad on booze.

At midnight he left the party still in full swing and stumbled to his vehicle. Finding the lock at the third attempt, twinkle-toes poured himself into the driver's seat and cautiously set off.

The roads were deserted and by the time he reached the motorway he was feeling more his old self again. Speeding along in the outside lane he noticed some roadworks coming up. For some reason, due no doubt to the Latin American syncopations still pulsating round his head, he decided to do a slalom round the road cones.

Amazingly, he didn't hit any of the cones and, tiring of that manoeuvre, he switched to the snow plough and flattened a full five miles' worth of cones before the police pulled him over.

The inebriate hoofer threw himself at the officers' mercy, telling them his whole sorry tale, and how he'd never transgressed before.

He was a pitiful sight, grovelling for leniency, and the officers' fierce demeanour softened. So much so, in fact, that they relented, saying, 'Right then sir, put every single cone back where it was, and we'll let you off with a caution.'

Technophobia

* In the fifties, when built-in obsolescence was endemic, Cadillacs had a special zip fitted in the door panels. When it was pulled, it scratched the metal, thus encouraging rust

* British cars (remember them?) often had special pockets in the wheel arches designed to catch mud and make the bodywork rust

* Scientists have invented a car that runs on water, but all the world's oil companies have got together, paid off the scientists involved, and are keeping it under wraps

* A woman on the Essex coast has an everlasting light bulb burning in her porch which got mixed into a batch of ordinary bulbs by mistake. The company who made it keep trying to buy it back, but she won't sell

* Japanese computers are aware when the guarantee runs out

* Computers never actually forget anything that's accidentally lost, it's just that you have to be an expert to get at all the information

* One of the new hospital trusts tried to avoid the pernicious Michelangelo computer virus by scrolling the calendar on their network past the date when the virus

was due to be activated, but as they passed the date, the virus was activated and all the medical records on their system were lost

* Putting bigger wheels on the back of your car means you're always going downhill, thus saving petrol

* The journey from Edinburgh to London is shorter than the other way round, because it's all downhill

* A car's hubcap once spun off and decapitated a dog on the pavement

* Mix iron filings into a car body repair and the magnet will stick when someone's testing it

* An electrical storm once happened while pupils at an American school were taking a maths exam. All their calculators went haywire and every single child failed

the long *arm of the law*

Scams and scamsters

Crime doesn't pay ... enough. Judge for yourself. This roll call of scams and scamsters points the finger at those who have a stab at the things we'd all secretly love to get away with. But if you're dumb enough to try some of the ill-conceived schemes here, remember: ignorance really is no defence.

signed, *sealed and delivered*

The father of a bloke I went to school with was a sergeant in the Sweeney – or so he said – and was once called out to the scene of an armed robbery, a high street bank.

The teller explained a shifty-looking bloke in a trench-coat had entered the bank, come over to his window and shoved a dog-eared envelope under the glass.

The bank clerk squinted at the childish scrawl on the back of the envelope. The note read, 'GIV US ALL THE MUNNY, IVE GOT A GUN'.

He looked up to find himself staring point-blank down the barrel of a shaking pistol. Normally a stickler for company guidelines, the teller complied immediately, thrusting wads of tenners over the counter, which the robber thrust into his greedy holdall.

Meanwhile, the thief himself had just arrived home and started excitedly to count his booty, when the police burst through the door bristling with automatic weapons.

The robber threw his arms in the air immediately, but was baffled by the efficiency of the police on the case. 'How did you track me down so fast?' he wailed.

'Quite simple, Mastermind,' the sergeant sneered, snapping on the bracelets. 'Your name and address were on the other side of the envelope.'

This sorry tale of criminal negligence is similar in some ways to the tale of the motorcycle courier who unknowingly delivers a stick-up note and is promptly arrested – we included that one in the previous book.

It seems that criminal minds are always on the

look-out for business opportunities. Not content with ripping off the post office, they even pick on such unlikely targets as the poor and old-age pensioners. But that's enough about the government. There seems to be no situation which the human mind cannot corrupt, as this series of scams and scamsters illustrates . . .

return *to sender*

The friend of a fellow who frequents the local pub works for the Royal Mail in the East End of London. His post office is on a bleak concrete estate of graffiti-spattered tower blocks.

The post office was pretty quiet. Locals tended to pop in for the odd second-class stamp, or the occasional TV licence. But for some strange reason recorded delivery was very popular.

People would use it mostly to return goods, especially hi-fi systems, that they had ordered from mail-order catalogues, but for some reason had found unsatisfactory.

Oddly, many of these items failed to turn up at their destination, and one particular catalogue company was forever claiming on the post office's insurance for the missing property. Immediately suspecting bent posties on the fiddle, the caring management sent in a team of undercover snoopers.

They were all shocked by the cunning scam they unearthed. The locals had been returning their unwanted goods by recorded delivery, filling in the catalogue company's address on the slip and getting it stamped, but using their own address as the return address.

The counter staff had failed to notice the discrepancy, and the stolen goods were being delivered to the con-merchants' abodes safe and sound the very next day.

a matter *of trust*

An acquaintance works in the City of London in an exclusive franchise operation. To maximise working hours and quality time, as befits an executive mover and shaker of her standing, she retains a penthouse apartment in the Barbican, a brisk clatter of heels from her workplace.

One day, two tradesmen called into her office explaining that they were working in the area laying carpet.

Apparently, they were kitting out large hotels in the locality, and due to an oversight had a couple of rolls of premium quality 100 per cent wool Axminster available at a 'giveaway' rate.

In her flat she'd previously opted for a good, long-lasting shag on the floor, but she was seduced by the rich blue tufted-twist sample, and loved the rock bottom price even more.

Never a Ms to miss a bargain, and gradually convincing herself that her present carpeting was a little worn, she asked them how soon the lay could be completed. They said it could be 'same-day', so she gave the fitters her house keys and the requisite cash.

Finishing work on time for a change, she dashed back, keen to view the new floor.

But when she swung the door open, she was appalled

to see acres of truly top-notch carpet sporting a large white 'Trust House Forte' logo every few yards.

foul *play*

A mate who began work in Docklands during the construction explosion of the eighties was regaled with the story of one of his predecessors who laboured in the area when it was still used to offload goods from the world's ships, and not to load the wallets of the world's shits.

Apparently, this young apprentice also played for the works football team, and one Saturday, in a particularly rough match with another dockers' team, he was clobbered with a studs-up tackle by the opposition's hatchet man for being flash.

Writhing in agony, the players soon realised that the lad's shin was badly broken. One docker immediately began to run for an ambulance, but some of the older, wiser lags had a better idea and called him back.

They got the wounded boy standing again, helped him home, and told him to hold his leg until Monday, which he did. When Monday arrived, they carried him painfully into work, placed him at the bottom of a big grain silo, and ran for the foreman, claiming the lad was the victim of an industrial accident.

It worked – and the young man received £10,000 in compensation.

crisp *business*

A small crisp factory in the Midlands was suffering from such a cashflow crisis that they could barely even afford to buy the spuds that were their lifeblood.

Then in a flash of brilliance one young shopfloor scamster hit upon a wizard scheme to save the day. Without wasting any time, the company acted on his initiative and launched a high-profile nationwide 'Interesting Potato' competition, asking entrants to send them as many funny-shaped, comical, odd or lewdly-knobbled spuds as they could.

Strangely, there was no prize given out. But all the entries were turned into crisps and the factory made a small fortune.

fitted up *wardrobe*

A bloke who lives round the corner left his keys with a neighbour while he and his family went on holiday to Frinton.

The neighbour, a conscientious chap, was a credit to the Neighbourhood Watch, and took his responsibility very seriously, keeping a weather eye on the property at all times.

When a furniture van turned up on the Wednesday to deliver a new wardrobe, the curtain-twitcher diligently let them in, signed for the furniture, and kept an eye on the deliverymen while they were inside the property.

They seemed pleasant enough chaps, if a little dense – he wasn't really surprised when they turned up again the next day saying they'd delivered the wrong piece and would have to take it back. He left them to it, watched them leave, and again locked up carefully.

But when the family returned from down south, they found everything they had – video, TV, jewellery, micro-wave – was missing.

The police arrived and questioned the neighbour intensely. He wracked his brains but could recall nothing out of the ordinary apart from the slight problem with the wardrobe.

The officers nodded knowingly. 'They're pulling that one all over town,' they explained.

Apparently, a diminutive villain hides in the wardrobe when it's delivered. Then he fills it up with consumer collectables overnight, and his accomplices remove him and the booty along with the 'wrong' wardrobe the next day.

take *the tube*

An old friend now living in London used to run a pub in Dublin. It was a typically lively, bustling bar where the crack was always good and the Guinness flowed like – well, like Guinness in a Dublin bar really.

Anyhow, one day, after a particularly heavy lunchtime session, the landlord went to switch on the racing and noticed to his dismay that the TV had been stolen from its shelf up on the wall. Straight away he got on the blower to the 'Gards' and within a few minutes two officers arrived.

Officiously noting down various interior details, the sergeant finally approached the landlord and asked where the goggle box was when it was stolen.

The landlord pointed to the empty shelf high up on the wall.

'Well, it's people like you who make our job impossible,' groaned the sergeant. 'Fancy leaving an expensive article like that out where everyone can see it.'

an unfair *cop*

A friend's dad is a desk sergeant in the West Midlands Constabulary. Although his job these days is a long way from the frontline in the fight against crime, in his younger days he pounded the beat around Handsworth.

This was well before the days of joyriders, ramraiders and serial killers: criminals in those days were an altogether nicer breed. At the time one of his colleagues had an interesting experience. The copper was patrolling a particularly ill-lit street. With his torch blazing, he flashed into each doorway and ginnel, weeding out the homeless and stopping every black BMW he saw, and generally keeping 'em peeled.

It was just as well, because his vigilance soon paid off. The flashlight illuminated the front of a cosy old tobacconist's with the door slightly ajar.

Steeling himself for possible violent confrontation, he slowly pushed open the door. Nothing appeared to be amiss, so radioing the station the flatfoot poked around the shop. Then he checked no one was looking and helped himself to 200 cigarettes, which he hid under his helmet.

The flustered shopowner arrived shortly, bursting with gratitude, and after checking his goods he praised the policeman's diligence and dedication to the job. Then he

insisted on giving the officer a little 'thank you' for his trouble. 'Here, take these two hundred ciggies,' he offered.

'No, no, sir that really won't be necessary, I'm only doing my job,' the bobby protested uncomfortably. 'Anyway, I don't have anywhere to put them.'

'Nonsense,' replied the shopkeeper, reaching up. 'You can hide them under your helmet.'

the quite *good Samaritan*

A friend of a friend who worked in a video shop in Leicester was walking along the high street one lunchtime to pay in the previous night's takings when he was taken by surprise by a mugger who grabbed his bag. As he was about to react, he felt the cold stab of steel in his stomach and fell down in a heap to the horror of passers-by, who formed a typically British crowd round him, staring and tut-tutting.

Half-conscious and lying in a rapidly increasing pool of blood on the pavement, the victim looked to be on the way out unless someone acted quickly, and it happened that a young man drawn to the commotion burst through the crowd and took control. He tore open the bleeding man's shirt, reached into his own pocket and pulled out an American Express card, which he promptly held over the wound – a tip you learn from first-aid classes, apparently.

This staunched the flow of blood until the ambulance arrived ten minutes later, but when the good Samaritan saw a police car bringing up the rear, he sharply directed a bystander to take over holding the card and hastily burst through the crowd, tearing away down the street.

Naturally, when he'd recovered, the stabbing victim wanted to reward the mystery man who'd saved his life, and sought the assistance of the police in the matter. But when he asked at the station, he got a bit of a surprise.

The sergeant explained that the police themselves had tried to trace the other fellow to return the American Express card. But their enquiries ground to a halt immediately – a routine check revealed that the Amex had been reported stolen just an hour before it was used as a life-saver.

who guards *the guard dog?*

A retail warehouse in chirpy cockney East London was packed to the rafters with reconditioned televisions, but had been broken into so often that the owners were forced to consider security measures.

The boss, not normally one to throw money at a problem, knew that peace of mind didn't come cheap and resolved to dig deep. He looked in *Yellow Pages* and found the largest, most ferocious guard dog in the area to protect the premises. Half Rottweiler, half timber wolf, half grizzly (three halves – we told you it was big), the watchdog cost him an arm and a leg (not literally, you understand – the dog was well disciplined).

The beast was a great success. There were no more break-ins and the company was the envy of other local businesses, so secure was their yard, and so intelligent was their hound.

Then one morning the boss arrived at 8.30 as usual, and noticed that the front gate had been forced. He anxiously called for his trusty cur, but it was nowhere to be seen. Scrupulously checking over all his stock the boss discovered that nothing had been stolen – except the invaluable guard dog.

> Definitely approaching 'classic' status, that hoary old tale. Some versions suggest it's a domestic house protector. But always nothing is stolen except the dog. If you don't have a dog and still nothing is stolen when there's a break-in, you've really got problems . . .

pipe *down*

One night, a mate was woken from his sleep by an awful crunching sound, then a horrible dull thud. He jumped out of bed, opened the window and looked into the street to see what had happened.

To his surprise, when he leaned out, he could see a drainpipe hanging off at right-angles from his house. Then he heard a mournful groaning and could just make out in the lamplight a hunched figure in the shrubbery clutching his head.

The would-be burglar looked up at him in the open window, and after a moment shouted, 'Sorry about your drainpipe!' before hobbling off into the night.

un-des-*irable*

A bloke at work wasn't looking forward to his fiftieth birthday, and was even more upset at some of the cards he got – all the usual 'over the hill/past it', 'a man is only as old as the woman he feels' jokes.

The presents he received from his workmates were even more irritating – an inflatable walking stick, a pair of plastic incontinence pants and, pick of the bunch, a CD of Des O'Connor's greatest hits.

He was a great music lover and proud of his collection, so this was a real insult. Without removing the disc from its shrink-wrap, he went down to the local record shop with the disc hidden in his pocket.

Then he looked around to make sure no-one was looking and lifted the item out of his pocket. He was about to put it back on the rack when a security man pounced, accusing him of shoplifting.

But within a few minutes, he was let off without charge – it would have been laughed out of court. After all, who would genuinely wish to steal something sung by Des O'Connor?

trial *by* *TV*

At our local pub in Wythenshawe a bloke came in one evening claiming to work at a local electrical manufacturer.

He said they were selling off a couple of hundred teletext TV sets and he was able to sell them factory fresh from the back of his lorry, dirt cheap. All hush-hush, you understand.

In fact, he said, he could get any electrical stuff to order – all you had to do was put your name and address down on his list and say what you wanted him to get hold of.

The news spread around other pubs in the area like wildfire, and after a few days there were a number of people awaiting delivery of some illicit consumer electronics.

Apparently, neither the mystery vendor nor any of the stuff ever appeared, but one by one all who'd put their name down on the dratted list had their collar felt by plod for handling stolen goods.

> That one's a clear adaptation of real life. Remember those FBI round-ups in the USA where they sent hundreds of elusive hoods tickets to glamorous receptions to 'Meet the Mets' etc, then when the last nogoodnik had arrived, they'd lock the doors and arrest the lot of 'em? In the UK, when

CB radio was a widespread but illegal practice, word had it that the DTI (watchdogs of the airwaves) would pretend to be 'good buddies', arrange for an 'eyeball', or face-to-face meeting, and slap on the bracelets when they met up.

Still on a nostalgia kick, it's good to see seventies style, and platform shoes in particular, back in fashion – and with them all the usual batch of consumer myths.

soled *out*

Just recently, a thrusting nineties entrepreneur stallholder in Islington, north London, keen to cash in on the latest revival, found a cheap source of platform shoes.

He knew a nice little earner when he saw one, and knew

the local yuppies would jump on any bandwagon going. The clogs weren't amazingly new – in fact they looked as though they'd survived in a time warp from the last fad in the early seventies. But the price was right – dirt cheap – and there were left *and* right shoes (unlike some he'd heard had been bought not long ago). So he parted with the ackers and pushed them out to the punters for a monkey a pair (£20 to you, madam).

But his success was shortlived. Soon disgruntled purchasers began returning the stack-heels and demanding their money back.

When he inspected them, the stallholder saw that the ancient heels were riddled with woodworm, and collapsed into dust as soon as any weight was put on them.

a crushing *blow*

A real wide boy in an Exeter market was doing a roaring trade with a huge batch of crushed down quilts he'd acquired.

But his luck was out when Trading Standards officers masquerading as punters bought a king-size duvet and examined the filling, finding it not to be costly down at all, but dirt-cheap polyester.

The next Saturday, the council officers found the bloke at his usual pitch and presented him with the evidence, pointing to his 'Crushed Down Doovays' sign and accusing him of knowingly misleading the public.

But the bloke protested his innocence: 'Of course they're crushed down,' he protested; 'how else would I have got all this lot in my estate?'

duvet *bugs*

A young housewife was keen to modernise her home and one morning when her husband was at work she bought their very first duvet and cover.

It looked absolutely smashing, although she found it a little heavier than she expected, and hard to smooth out properly. When later she found herself near the local market she'd bought it from, she asked the shifty market trader about the quilt's lumpy appearance. He replied it was down to 'settling', and being a quilt novice she believed him.

However, when she went to admire it again later, she was concerned to find it twitching on the floor.

Putting her fears aside, the young woman warily slit open a corner and peered inside, only to discover a seething sea of maggots.

They were all gorging themselves on the fleshy remnants on the feather shafts of the cheap filling.

> Ah, duvets. Treated with derision by the older generation when they came out ('They're murder to tuck in!'), they've superseded curtains as the innocent household accoutrement most likely to harbour purest insect evil. If you've come across our first book, *Healey & Glanvill's Urban Myths*, you'll know the story about the tarantulas in the Marks & Spencer yucca plant. Recent variations suggest that when the 'men in coats' fumigate the plant, they only find the male spider, and immediately set about finding his mate – 'they're never far away'. They find the female spider: a) in the duvet cover; or b) in the baby's cot duvet;

but always surrounded by a clutch of hundreds
of baby tarantulas.

off the *back of a lorry*

A bloke I met at a swanky top people's dinner party in
Bow knew about some lucky villains who'd had a very
close shave. The criminals were going to rip off the local
Currys electrical warehouse, and stole a large white van fit
for their purpose.

Round the back of the store the yard was floodlit, but
the cheeky crooks took no heed, jemmied the roller shutter,
backed up, and started shifting gear.

They'd half filled the van when a panda car on routine
patrol came round the corner. Quick as a flash, the robbers
started unloading the boxes back into the store. The cops
took one look and, thinking it was a late delivery, gave a
cheery wave and drove on.

reds *in the Fed*

A German dentist acquaintance tells me that a strange
phenomenon has recently occurred in his newly reunited
country.

Apparently Russian citizens from Boris Yeltsin's new
market capitalist states have been crossing the border into
former East Germany under cover of darkness.

Once there, the ex-Communists have been committing
minor crimes with the aim of deliberately having their
collars felt by Germany's rozzers, thereby being imprisoned
– the Russian villains have found out they can earn far

more hard currency in Germany's liberal prison schemes than they can back home.

> The only reservation we have about that one concerns the fact that Russian police cars aren't anywhere near as fast as the local gangsters' expensive getaway vehicles – and state-imposed frugality means they aren't given enough petrol to chase them in the first place. Not a place yer typical larcenist would be desperate to leave, now is it? Apparently the new privatised services aren't much better either. When a Moscow friend's sink sprang a leak and he rang the local plumber, the workman arranged to come round but said he was booked up until two years three weeks on Wednesday after lunch. 'Oh dear,' said the friend, 'can you make it the morning because I've got the gas man coming round in the afternoon.'

blue *murder*

A small-time Cardiff TV company a friend used to work for was very excited one day when they landed something of a scoop. There had been a grisly death of a woman in the locality and the chief of police in Wales had agreed to be interviewed for HTV – a very rare occurrence, and one which showed how seriously the law was taking the crime.

The hand-picked outside broadcast crew arrived on location, set up, and respectfully greeted the stuffy big-wig, who was clearly deeply affected by what he'd witnessed in the house.

The interview was understandably solemn as the police chief relayed the details of the horrible death in a dignified monotone:

'Several parts of the woman's body, including the head, were found by officers in the fridge; both legs and one arm were discovered in the potting shed, and the bulk of the torso was uncovered by police digging in the flower beds,' explained the pallid chief.

At the end of the interview, the producer thanked him in hushed tones, and the crew stood in respectful silence.

All except the sound engineer, that is, who immediately chirruped: 'So you've ruled out suicide then?'

myth*ellaneous*

Legal

✻ Manufacturers could make cars that were impossible to break into and steal, but they won't do it because write-offs help sales

✻ With a telephone card and a teaspoon, a talented thief can infiltrate any establishment in the country

✻ There's a code you can punch in on your telephone that will make all your calls free from then on. When people are caught doing it, they're charged with another crime and it's all hushed up

✻ Buy stamps with '1st Class' on them now and because of inflation they'll be worth millions in years to come

✻ Music-loving Colombians are furious at a drug smuggler who pressed cocaine into a record and got caught by customs at Heathrow – every record coming in from the country is now split open

✻ Before the Prime Minister visited a national newspaper recently, police sniffer dogs found no guns or explosives – but a huge stash of marijuana in the toilets

✻ If you want to hide the corpse after a murder, give it to a pig. They eat the lot – even the toenails

food *and drink*

Half-baked hiccups

Eat, drink and be wary. The daily bread's mouldy, the milk of human kindness is curdled, and even the pint that thinks it's a quart isn't quite so sure any more. A gut-rotting helping of scare-stories and indigestible suggestions, spiced up with lashings of sauce . . .

one *lump or two?*

A deeply religious mother of seven in rural Killarney had nagged her workshy husband into redecorating the entire house in honour of the 'Stations of the Cross' ceremony.

The exterior of the small terrace was freshly painted and the inside spring-cleaned with a vengeance.

The woman decided to top it all off by asking the local priest round to afternoon tea. The venerable cleric was happy to fit the date into his busy schedule and looked forward to the Sunday afternoon, as the woman was a renowned cook and a generous host.

When the day dawned everything was in order: best china, lace tablecloth and a choice of three different fancy cakes all laid out with a vase of flowers in the front parlour.

Sadly it was a rainy day and all the kids were playing merry hell in the house. Worst of all they kept running into the front room and pinching the sugar lumps from the tea set.

The mother collared the youngest, giving him a firm clip round the ear and snatching the half empty sugar bowl from his sticky grip, only then discovering to her horror it had been smashed in two.

It was just at that point the doorbell rang. More than a little flustered, the woman quickly picked up the sugar lumps, and to keep them out of harm's way stuffed them into her ample cleavage. The smiling priest commented on how nice the house was looking and, nibbling a slice of Madeira, made all the right noises about her proficiency in the kitchen. Then as she poured his tea, not spotting a sugar bowl, the priest asked, 'Do you have any sugar?'

Without thinking the woman fished a few lumps out of her cleavage. Then she innocently asked, 'Milk, Father?'

'No, No!' exclaimed the priest, leaping to his feet . . .

when *men were men*

Up in Cumbria, Cumberland as 'twas in the heady days of the early 1950s, a woman's place was in the home and a man's place was any place he chose – and he usually chose the pub. Nowadays, thank goodness, things are much different.

But let's roll back the years for a moment to a time when this mate of a friend's dad would prop up the bar of the local Working Men's Club until closing, then teeter home several sheets to the wind.

His long-suffering wife was fond of an early night, but stupidly she would always leave the boozer something for his supper in the kitchen – she'd obviously never heard of the old adage: 'Keep 'em lean, keep 'em keen.'

One night the stop-out was setting out for the club as usual when his wife shouted from the kitchen that she'd leave out some fresh fish for him to cook up when he got back.

In the wee small hours, he stumbled in in his normal inebriated state, lit the gas, stumbled around for the fish and wolfed it down – it barely touched the sides.

The following morning, as the bloke settled down behind his breakfast paper, his wife asked him why he'd decided not to eat the smashing cod fillet she'd left for him the night before.

Confused, the bloke assured her that he had eaten the fish, and very tasty it was too. When his wife produced the fillet intact, he was flummoxed.

But he never did see his flat cloth cap again.

> Which reminds us of the other drunk on his way home from the pub, whose flat cap fell off in a cow field. He tried on twenty others before he found the right one.

you *must be choking*

An old friend of my auntie who works as a hospital cleaner was flicking his mop around casualty when a man was hurriedly stretchered in clutching his throat and coughing violently. The curtains were pulled and a junior doctor dashed breathlessly to the bedside, but there was just enough of a gap for the orderly to eavesdrop and catch a glimpse of what occurred.

The doctor carefully opened the man's mouth, manipulated his forceps, and removed a tightly wedged obstruction. Then he examined it closely as the patient recovered with an antiseptic gargle.

'What were you eating when you started to choke?' asked the doctor.

The patient croaked that he'd been enjoying a portion of southern-fried chicken.

'Well, well,' continued the medic – whose brother was of course a vet – 'unless I'm very much mistaken, I've just removed a cat's collarbone from your windpipe.'

> The cat's bone choker story follows a perennially common theme, and should really be told with a multiple-choice facility – choose from 'southern-fried chicken', the 'local Indian', the 'new Chinese' – with an instruction to delete according to prejudice.

locust *pastie*

A famished vegetarian at a small rock festival in Northumberland was pleased to see the sign above a burger van advertising veggie pasties, and without more ado bought and tucked into one.

But after just a few mouthfuls, her expression changed and she spat out what looked like a piece of some beanstalk.

One of her hippy friends was a keen nature lover, and

after a closer inspection, pronounced the foreign body a well-masticated but still identifiable locust's leg.

frank*hurter*

A keen young butcher's assistant in Bangor was required to carry out the regular task of collecting all the offcuts of pork and feeding them through the mincer to make a huge string of sausages.

One day, he was absently forcing down an especially tough piece of gristle when he became aware that his hand was more than usually deep in the workings of the machine.

Immediately withdrawing his arm, he was horrified to see that the sharp mashing mechanism had removed his hand without him even noticing.

The butcher dispatched him off to hospital, but being thrifty, still put the batch of sausages on sale – and several regular customers commented on how nice they were.

family *concern*

A classy new Chinese restaurant in Chelmsford produced spicy meatballs that were the envy of all rivals in the district, and no one was able to match the recipe, which the owner refused to divulge.

Whenever asked, he would tap his nose, lean over and say conspiratorially, 'Recipe of old England'. But it was clearly the meat and not the spices which held the key.

As it turned out, this wasn't too surprising. Over a period of weeks, a suspicious rival observed the restaurant owner's brother bringing in consignments of meat at night, and the police were called in – the brother happened to work at a nearby cemetery.

gums *and plums*

A young woman from Northampton, excited about some new imported Chinese bubble gum boasting an everlasting chew, found to her delight that you could masticate for hours and still have something substantial in your mouth.

Her health-conscious parents had always warned her against swallowing, because as we all know ingesting chewing gum gives you worms, so when her jaw got too achy, she spat the gum out into the foil it came in.

But looking down she was horrified to see the gum had a recognisable shape to it, and one that she was familiar with: apparently each piece of the everlasting gum contained a condom.

cream *tea-leaf*

A friend of my girlfriend's mother is a retired school teacher. She lives in an idyllic rose-covered cottage in the Yorkshire dales.

She often motors to upmarket Harrogate in her trusty vintage Morris Minor for her provisions. A pension doesn't go far these days, and after a few purchases, she tends to spend the remainder of the day window shopping. As a special treat, money permitting, she sometimes takes tea at one of the more genteel establishments.

One afternoon, she was especially looking forward to her cup of speciality tea – refreshing Earl Grey – and called into her usual tiffin haunt, but the place was filled to the rafters with the rowdy antiques fair crowd.

The waitress was rather embarrassed at having to sideline a regular customer (even if she wasn't a big spender) but offered the upright ma'am a space if she didn't mind sharing.

Disappointed, but gagging for a cuppa, the elderly lady reluctantly agreed and was led to a small window table opposite a gent in tweed jacket and leather elbow patches. The chap smiled politely, then returned to his book. After a few minutes he upped and left.

Sipping tea from her china cup the old lady couldn't help noticing that the fellow hadn't eaten his inviting jam doughnut. Feeling a bit peckish after her hard afternoon's perambulations, she eyed it hungrily. It seemed such a shame to waste it.

She was just finishing off the doughnut, stuffing it into her mouth in a most unladylike fashion, when the gentleman returned to the table, having bought himself a fresh cup of tea.

> Very similar to the classic mistaken Kit-Kat story
> (*see* **Urban Classics**: Take a break) in the way
> the yarn plays on manners and that great British
> fear, the *faux pas*, though with a different twist
> and satisfying pay-off.

norra *lorra luck*

A friend from Wigan often eats out in the local Italian nosheteria, Don Corleone's Pizza Shop, and was once lucky enough to witness a strange occurrence there.

As usual the place – a mere ten-minute joyride from Liverpool – was crammed with scousers. One couple, sporting matching mauve shell-suits, were going for the works: prawn cocktail, garlic bread (minus the garlic), gutbuster pizzas and black forest gateau, washed down with pints of house vino.

'Vino collapso, eh luv?' the young bloke quipped, as the owner brought them their bill.

Suspicions were aroused when the perm-haired scouser didn't pay with the usual fistful of crumpled tenners, but offered a credit card. The restaurateur took one look at the flexible friend and ordered his head waiter, 'Call the police!'

'What's wrong?' asked the scally. 'Why can't I pay with the card?'

'Because,' replied the owner, blocking the door, 'this is my card – it was stolen from my wallet last week.'

For another scurrilous credit card rumour with a happier ending see The quite good Samaritan in the **Long Arm of the Law** section.

stake*out*

A mate of my dad's drinks out at a country pub in Norfolk. The place is well off the beaten track, and most of the regulars drive down there from all over the shop, often motoring home well in excess of the legal limit.

The local constabulary got wise to the flagrant flouting of the drink-driving law by the pub's patrons, and, needing to boost their monthly arrest rate anyway, decided to stake out the pub. That night a panda car hid in the bushes across the road from the boozer and waited. Over the next few weeks, they rounded up and charged drink-drivers spilling out of the pub nearly every night.

Then one night just before closing time, with the panda car lurking out of sight opposite the boozer as usual, a regular tippler, apprehended by the police a few days earlier, stumbled out and wobbled over to his vehicle, slurring Rod Stewart's 'D'Ya Think I'm Sexy' at the top of his voice. Then he fell over, struggled to find his feet, and spent a fruitless ten minutes trying to locate the keyslot to unlock his motor. Eventually he managed by holding the handle with one hand, shutting one eye, and sliding his key down his arm into the slot.

Two confident coppers witnessed the whole sorry affair from their car and chuckled to each other, 'We've got a right one here.'

The bloke set off with a screech and kangarooed down the road before switching his lights on. Sirens wailing, the filth set off in hot pursuit, flashed their lights and, after he'd eluded them with a series of late turns, finally pulled the erratic driver over.

The smirking rozzers swaggered out of their car metaphorically rubbing their hands with glee. The bloke wound his window down slowly and with perfect enunciation said, 'Is there a problem officer? What seems to be the matter?'

The breathalyser revealed he was stone cold sober. Realising they'd been stung by a decoy, the cops raced back to the pub. But the car park was now empty, and the locals had all made their way home unharassed.

a sour *note*

A friend of a friend from East Anglia once knew a real skinflint who used to drink in the same local. The cheapskate always arrived at half past eight, regular as clockwork, ordered his pint of bitter, perched on his favourite stool, and saw out the rest of the evening without further troubling the bar staff. Such behaviour not only irritated the landlord, a batey fellow at the best of times, but also got the goat of the other regulars, especially as the parsimonious bloke was so smug about his thriftiness and immune to any ribbing.

There was only one way the others in the local could

get back at the miserly imbiber. When he slipped off his stool to visit the toilet, one of the other drinkers would nip over and enjoy a large gulp of his warm beer. When the bloke came back from the urinal, he would explode to see his carefully nursed pint depleted in his absence, and harangue the whole bar, shouting and stabbing his finger, 'Who's bin at my pint? It were you, weren't it!'

Apparently this had gone on for some months, when one night the penny-pincher came up with an answer to deter any would-be surreptitious slurpers. When he went to the toilet, he stuck a little note by his pint, which said: 'I've spit in this!' But when he returned from his micturition he found his note slightly amended; next to 'I've spit in this!', some anonymous rogue had scrawled 'So have I!'

myth*ellaneous*

Consumption

✳ Statistically, vegetarians are more likely to meet a violent death

✳ Beefburgers are often a whole flame-grilled cow cyst with all the trimmings

✳ They tried unsuccessfully to launch 'kangaburgers' in Australia. When cooked, worms would come crawling out – kangaroos are riddled with them. As are cod

✳ Don't order 'long pig' or 'two-legged pork' in China

✳ Blue 'Smarties' and green 'M&Ms' are aphrodisiacs

✳ 'Space Dust', a children's sweet from the eighties, was withdrawn because it was really a hallucinogenic drug

✳ Orange juice is the single largest cause of lethargy in the Western world

✳ Students often find worms in their staple diet – cans of tomatoes

✳ Packets of a certain type of cigarette have 'KKK' in their design, because the company supports white supremacists

✳ A big hamburger chain gives a percentage of its profits to the IRA; the same company is the world's largest purchaser of factory-farmed earthworms . . .

international *incidents*

Fabulous foreign affairs

The British aren't the only gullible and superstitious people in the world, as this litany of local stories culled from the five corners of the earth sadly attests. And if there also happens to be a foreign tourist involved, it's cheap thrills, cheap jibes and cheap laughs all the way. Got the travel bug? Swat it.

the Mexican *tobacco pouch*

Back in the swinging sixties a friend of a friend in the printing trade knew a sales executive who worked for a large North American paper company.

The salesman had just returned home after travelling around Central America flogging his wares for three months. His wife seemed very pleased to see him back in one piece and after a happy reunion she fixed him a drink and told him to relax while she unpacked his case.

He'd just settled back down in the settee when his loved one appeared at the door holding a heavy duty contraceptive sheath (they were reusable in those days), and demanded to know what it was. Spluttering into his drink, the bloke's mental processes worked like lightning.

'It's a souvenir,' he blustered. 'In fact, it's a Mexican tobacco pouch.' Happy with the explanation the wife toddled off to finish her chores.

The bloke thought nothing more of the incident until a few months later when he was travelling down through South America. It was approaching Thanksgiving and he was feeling a little homesick, so he sent a message down the wire saying he was taking time off for a surprise visit home.

The worried boss telexed back, 'MEXICAN TOBACCO POUCH ON SALE AT CHURCH BAZAAR. STOP. SUGGEST YOU KEEP ON TRAVELLING. STOP.'

This yarn is a real salesman-in-the-pub's 'only in America' shaggy dog story, an old, old classic that seems to have fallen into disuse. We are pledged to putting it back up there where it belongs. The poor old Yanks do seem to come in for some unflattering mythological criticism. See below . . .

very *disturbed*

A friend of a friend who worked as a receptionist in one of London's swankiest hotels had a low opinion of most people, and when you hear some of his tales, you can understand why.

Once he was looking after a motley bunch of rich mid-western Americans who'd arrived on a 'heritage' tour. Most of them had never been out of Alabama, let alone stayed in a hotel, and London was a wondrous thing to them – if a little busy, new-fangled and intimidating.

Pretty soon the bloke realised such an unworldly bunch was going to be hard work, and suggested that they all go to their rooms first, freshen up, then come down in an hour for a welcome meeting.

An hour later, all the rednecks had come downstairs to the lobby in their bright shorts and straw hats, already pointing the camcorder at everyone and everything. All except one old lady, that is, who failed to show. After another half hour, the receptionist became concerned, so he rang the woman in her room. 'Oh! Ahm so glad y'awl cawled up,' she drawled tearfully. 'Ah cayn't get outa ma room.'

'Well, you just have to open the door and come down in the lift,' muttered the bloke.

But the woman was becoming hysterical and wouldn't listen to a word he said, just repeating that she couldn't get out of her room. Exasperated, the bloke ran upstairs to the woman's room, opened her door and walked in, pointing and saying, 'There, now that's what we in England call a door.'

But apparently the woman simply blubbed, 'But ah just simply could nawt go through that door.'

'Why ever not, madam?' sneered the bloke.

'Why, it has a sign saying "Do Not Disturb" hanging awn it.'

Australia – 'the land of plenty', 'down under'. The very words conjure up images of golden beaches, glorious sunshine, kangaroos bounding across the outback and beer-swilling macho men with corks on their hats. Australian society seems to have inherited all the characteristics of a myth-loving culture from its British criminal forebears: wanton gossip, outrageous lies and the tendency to drink to excess. In the previous book we mentioned the fashion-victim kangaroo that hopped off into the bush, and an unpleasant incident with a scorpion down under. Happily, we're now able to supply a further batch of Common-wealth imports . . .

the Aussie *flea-pit*

A friend from Doncaster recently went globetrotting and washed up in 'the land of plenty', Australia. The pommie traveller soon fell in with a goodtime hard-drinking crowd and spent day after day knocking back the Tooheys with the sheilas at the beach barbies.

But after a few months of the six-pack lifestyle, the tyke felt the pangs of cultural starvation, so he asked a woman he'd taken a shine to out to the cinema. She readily agreed and the couple, dressed in their best singlets and shorts, set out for *Mad Max 3*.

The picture palace was cool and dark after the roasting temperatures outside, and the girl led the way down the aisle as the Brit's eyes slowly adjusted to the gloom. She seemed to be marching to the front, even though there were plenty of seats closer to hand, so he plonked himself down at the end of a row and called her back.

Everyone in the cinema looked round and stared at him in amazement. The girl turned, saw where he was sitting, and rushed back flustered. She grabbed his arm, spitting at him, 'Are you mad? No one round here sits in the row-end seats! Didn't you hear about the escaped homicidal maniac who ran amok in a cinema and chopped off seven people's heads with a machete??!!'

measure *for measure*

A friend from Australia knows of a property developer in Sydney who bought one of two adjacent vacant plots in the expensive downtown business sector. The developer, who had a reputation as a sharp operator, hired a top architect and erected a huge state-of-the-art glass skyscraper.

Everything was going to plan, with tenants flooding in, when a thick manilla envelope thudded on to the developer's doormat. It was a solicitor's letter from the owner of

101

the adjacent plot, claiming that the new building encroached on his land by precisely one inch. An emergency surveyor was called, and after careful manipulation of the theodolite, his report showed the claim to be true.

The developer then tried to cut a deal to buy off the one-inch strip of land, but the asking price was astronomical – practically the same as he'd paid for the original site. So he wracked his brains for a cheaper way out, and finally hit on a drastic solution. Much to the amusement of the entire construction industry, he hired a team of men to grind the trespassing inch off his building.

The other plot owner was miffed to miss out on the windfall of the developer's error, but decided to erect his own edifice. So a few months later he built a glass tower of equal height and luxury butting right up against the first building.

No sooner was the office block finished than the owner of the first building sent out his own legal threat demanding massive compensation for this blatant encroachment on his land.

Apparently, the cunning fellow had ground not just one but two inches off his building.

child *hood*

A friend who's a disc jockey down under often travels to the fly-blown dustbowl towns of the outback as part of his job.

In one particular one-horse settlement, after a hard morning's chatshow blathering, the DJ took time off to visit a local watering hole, as was his habit.

He'd just gulped down the first draught of ice-cold amber nectar when an old sheep shearer sidled up to him.

'Here, you're that bloke on the radio, arncha?' he asked. The DJ nodded and the old cove continued.

'You see that bloke over in the corner?' The DJ nodded again, snatching a glance at a dishevelled barfly in a crumpled brown overcoat.

'Well, he used to be on the radio too. Sunday programme for kids it was. Went all over south Australia. He was a big family celebrity. Till one day he signed off at the end of the show and forgot to turn off his mike. Unknown to him his parting shot on the airwaves was, "Well, that's got rid of the little bastards, I'm off for a drink." And he hasn't worked since.'

when *in Rome*

A red-tape-loving chum who works for the EC in Brussels had to sort out a bureaucratic spat between the commission and the Italian government. Evidently Rome's rubber industry had been ordered to increase the size of Italian condoms, as they were failing to measure up to European norms.

This is strangely reminiscent of a story circulating after the Second World War. As part of the Marshall Plan to reconstruct the shattered German economy, the British government was shipping over essential supplies.

Churchill was well aware that the defeated populace had very little to occupy their time and, terrified of a post-war German population boom, he made sure the aid shipments included substantial quantities of condoms.

Never known to miss a propaganda initiative, though, the devious old bugger had the consignment made up of extra-large prophylactics, re-labelling the packets 'small' – a ploy bound to keep the Germans' morale low.

More recently a shipload of Japanese 'Johnnies' was sent back from Africa for failing to meet the exacting local requirements.

walt's *and all*

A nice family from Walsall arrived in Los Angeles for the holiday of a lifetime, with the delights of Disneyland at the top of their agenda.

The two young children – a sensible eight-year-old girl and a dozy boy of three – were understandably excited about the prospect of meeting Mickey, Donald and Tron face-to-face, not to mention the numerous death-defying rides in the pleasure park.

The day after they landed Stateside, the family made their first pilgrimage to the Walt Disney theme park.

After they'd been stung for the entry fee, the parents decided they'd done their bit and more or less left their kids to it, taking an easy stroll to just about keep up with them. After an hour of going on everything in sight, Mum and Dad thought it best to grab the kids and get them something to drink.

Their daughter was easily located, but the toddler appeared to have vanished into thin air.

The troubled parents immediately notified a security officer, who took their situation very seriously and swiftly led them to a central control unit crammed with banks of video security camera screens. The sobbing mother began blurting out, 'He's got blond hair . . .'

Gravely, the man in charge interrupted. 'We want you to forget what your son looked like, apart from his face. Just his features, that's all.'

Apparently, after a seemingly interminable ten minutes, the mother shouted that she thought she'd seen her little boy.

They zoomed the camera in to the face of a little child with black hair, holding the hand of a Mickey Mouse character, who was leading him towards the theme park's exit. As they watched, a group of security guards wrestled the Mickey Mouse figure to the ground and rescued the little boy. A little later, the family were reunited and the dye swiftly removed from the confused little lamb's hair.

Officials later admitted a gang of kidnappers for the slave trade in Colombia's cocaine industry were operating in the park.

However, the family were sworn to secrecy, paid off handsomely and given lifetime free entry to any Disney park in the world – an offer they've still to take up.

Given the concern of many people these days over a perceived increase in violence against children, it's rather odd that this 'white slave trade' myth should be so widespread at the moment. (Then again, myths have always displayed a nasty gallows humour.)

It's a tried and tested formula, with the Disney setting and characters, the dying of the hair, and the 'hushing up' – a common get-out employed by someone who's not too sure of the story themselves – now finding its voice in France with the arrival of EuroDisney. There's something people find irresistible about familiar and trustworthy figures being publicly debased in this way – that's why Parliament was invented.

divine *intervention*

A friend was told about an odd robbery that took place in the heart of the Bible belt in America's Deep South shortly before she arrived there.

Apparently, a bloke had walked into a hi-tech bank just before closing, pulled out a gun and said, 'This is a stick-up.' Everyone panicked and stood back until there was silence except for the cackle of a television in the corner of the room.

The robber was in the process of collecting all the money when suddenly the voice of a rabid evangelist on the TV shouted out for forgiveness and deliverance: 'Hallelujah!' The thief shut his eyes, raised his head heavenward and whispered 'Hallelujah'.

At which moment, suitably distracted, he was overpowered and held down till police arrived.

i wanna *be like you-oo-oo*

A bloke at the local pub was on holiday in Kuala Lumpur, Malaysia, with his wife. The two of them were having a smashing time until they were on a jungle walk and found themselves isolated from the rest of the party.

Suddenly a huge orang-utan emerged from the trees and

with force and dexterity stripped the bloke of all his clothes, before lumbering off, chattering excitedly, into the depths of the bush.

His wife wasn't touched, and gave him her fan to preserve his modesty.

> Holidays abroad are a rich area for urban myth-
> ology, and understandably so: you're in a strange
> place with odd customs and hidden horrors. By
> the time you've read these next few stories, you'll
> be tearing up your flight tickets.

alone *again, naturally*

A thoroughly respectable middle-aged couple from Reigate always enjoyed an annual holiday with a difference – they went to a naturist camp. One year the camp they chose was way down south on the Dalmatian coast in former Yugoslavia.

It involved a long journey in their trusty VW camper (with curtains), each taking turns to drive while the other slept in the back.

After a long sleep, the wife woke to find the mobile home at a standstill. Assuming they'd finally reached their destination, and still a little drowsy, she opened the door rubbing her eyes and stepped out of the van in her preferred state, utterly starkers.

She drew in a deep breath of fresh country air – and then choked on fumes.

The poor woman opened her eyes to see the camper

steaming off, leaving her naked at a busy city centre cross-roads, surrounded by curious, muttering Austrians.

the taste *of Greece*

The cousin of a friend was on a back-packing holiday around the Mediterranean and was having a smashing time travelling around the Greek islands – Asbestos, Domestos, Bilios, Chillisos, etc. (any more cheap cracks? – no, get on with the story) – until he fell asleep on the beach and woke to find his money and credit cards had been swiped.

The nearest place to get replacement cards and money sent out was a hydrofoil ride away; luckily he'd already booked the trip. So he suffered the whole journey with the lip-smacking smell of moussaka and stuffed vine leaves but no money to buy anything.

When he arrived at the bigger island, he found the bank was closed for lunch, so he tried to take his mind off food, and walked along the seafront.

Inevitably he came to a bar, and there at one of the tables was a queasy-looking Aussie bloke with a huge pile of spaghetti on a plate in front of him.

The back-packer stopped and looked. The pallid Aussie didn't look like he fancied it, and still hadn't touched the inviting pasta five minutes later.

So the starving traveller plucked up courage and approached him.

'Sorry to ask, mate, but I can't help noticing you haven't

touched your spaghetti. I'm starving – I've not had a thing
all day. D'you mind if I tuck into it?'

'Be my guest,' belched the Aussie. 'I've already eaten
it once.'

lava's *leap*

A young couple from Smethwick had a glorious wedding
and looked forward to the earth really moving on their
honeymoon – they'd booked into a romantic hotel on the
Canary Islands built next to an inactive volcano with a
glorious view of the sea.

On their first day, the newly-wed wife decided to have
a long bath, and her husband went for a quiet walk down
to the beach for a drink while she got herself ready for a
romp with her rampant man.

On his way back to the hotel, the lusty beau decided to take a short cut down a rough path he'd spied earlier. In the dusk it seemed to lead only as far as the hotel's fence.

So he vaulted the fence – and tumbled straight down the mouth of the volcano.

midnight *run*

Two friends from work went on holiday to the lovely Turkish holiday resort of Ephesus. The flight had arrived late, so on the first night they had their hotel meal and headed up to their separate adjoining bedrooms for an early night.

In the morning, one of them woke with the lark, looked out of the window at a cloudless sky, and filled with visions of the sea, sand and sights, dressed and knocked for his mate next door.

But when the door opened, it was a complete stranger who stood in his friend's room. The fellow spoke no English, but between them, they ascertained that the other Englishman was not in his room and that the new occupant had moved in that morning. The odd thing was, the room had also been redecorated too since last night.

The concerned man ran down to reception to find out if they knew what had happened – it wasn't like his friend to abscond without warning. At first the hotel receptionist suggested that he must be mistaken, saying no one had booked in with him, which didn't wash at all. Then, looking increasingly nervous, she explained that his companion had checked out first thing in the morning and gone to the airport.

Even more unconvinced, the bloke contacted the airline, who had no record of his friend travelling back, and then rang home to see if they'd heard anything. When all drew blanks, the suspicious bloke called in the police.

As it turned out, he did the right thing: the duty manager of the hotel broke down under questioning and admitted that the English guest had apparently contracted food poisoning from his evening meal, and had been so violently sick in his room that he had died.

They disposed of his body to cover up the incident, and repainted the room to cover their tracks, finally moving a new guest in to try to convince the dead man's friend that he was going mad.

Not every surprise in foreign climes will cost you your life, though.

underground *service*

A friend was in Moscow recently, and travelling on the marvellous and rather grand Russian metro system. What a pleasure it was, he was thinking, to have clean and efficient trains, a regular service and no worries about violence or muggings.

Then suddenly the carriage was invaded by a rough-looking leather-clad gang who guarded all exits to prevent the commuters leaving the carriage.

A man and a woman lay down on the carriage floor and made love in the full view of embarrassed passengers.

Those who turned their heads away had their faces pushed back to watch. A few minutes later the spectacle was over and the gang passed along the carriage demanding money for the show – five roubles each.

One elderly Muscovite protested that she couldn't afford five roubles, so the ruffians only charged pensioners three roubles each.

bun *voyage*

A friend's elderly English great-aunt lived in a rural part of Sierra Leone, a remnant of our glorious empire. But even more of a monument to our presence was the local post system – slow, bureaucratic and inefficient – and the woman knew this to her cost.

So when she decided to send her son back in England one of his favourite home-made cakes, she wrapped it up securely in brown paper, and went to the quiet post office suitably equipped with appropriate bribes.

She said to the man behind the counter that she wanted to make sure it was dispatched the same day so it didn't get stale, and he assured her it would be dealt with post-haste, accepting the substantial sum of money with a nod.

Relatively confident that her parcel would now be properly handled, the woman set off for home. A few moments later, she stopped short, remembering that she'd meant to send a telegram as well to wish her son a happy birthday.

But when the lady sauntered back into the post office, she was a little surprised to find the man who'd served her carefully cutting her cake into equal segments for the others in the office.

Africa is a hotbed of apocryphal storytelling, and

each new social event is the subject of rumour and counter rumour. HIV and AIDS, cutting such a swathe through African society, is a case in point. One persistent story, working its way around southern African society, concerns a group of embittered women, full-blown AIDS sufferers all, who are said to be taking it out on men, who they hold responsible for their situation, by carrying hypodermics to local night clubs and injecting unsuspecting ravers with their infected blood. Another concerns a UN officer (the UN are widely believed to have spread the AIDS virus around Africa) who dates a local woman. When his tour of duty finishes, he leaves her with a package 'not to be opened until I've gone'. The memento turns out to be a miniature coffin inscribed with the legend, 'Welcome to the world of AIDS.' (Numerous stories with similar twists exist. There's an Irish one: virgin is seduced on holiday by Italian dreamboat who gives her the same gift for her flight home. See our first book, *Urban Myths*, for a US version of the same story.)

overnight *bags*

In Zimbabwe, when a foreign head of state is due to visit (especially one with a fat cheque), Harare, the nation's capital, is temporarily transformed. Bunting, new statues and posters of the visiting dignitary appear, and the streets are 'cleansed' (i.e. anyone looking like a prostitute is picked up and detained by the police overnight).

In the late eighties, the then President of East Germany Erich Honecher was due to arrive for a brief stay. The bunting and posters went up, and the prostitutes (mostly Mozambicans, as the locals always claim) were rounded up.

Unfortunately, as one rumour had it, this particular time the Zimbabwean President Robert Mugabe's wife Sally was somehow mistakenly apprehended. Luckily the mistake was rectified before an international incident occurred.

However, one legacy of the round-up lingered. At the behest of the national health authority, all the ladies of the night were secretly tested for HIV during routine health check-ups.

After they were released, the figures showed that every single one of the women was HIV positive. A tragic revelation, and especially shocking for the many policemen who'd stood guard over the prostitutes during their stay in jail, and who'd taken advantage of their professional services overnight.

> Graham Hopwood, an urban mythologist at *The Namibian* newspaper, has noted the spread of another southern African legend. In the eighties, the American pulp TV series *Knight Rider* was shown in most southern African states. It featured a malevolent black combi van, and pretty soon spin-off reports started emerging of a deathly black combi that roved Namibia kidnapping children. This was adapted by South Africans shortly afterwards – the story there was that ambulances had been seen abducting black kids.

The myth was so rampant that for a short time crowds turned on ambulances they suspected of kidnapping, and in one incident in Soweto an ambulance was set upon and the driver killed.

hands *off*

A Ghanaian friend remembers a terrible scare story that circulated in waves all over west Africa for a time in the seventies, striking at the heart of the continent's social fabric.

He recalls that for a while it wasn't uncommon for people to avoid shaking hands, even though the handshake is one of the most routine greetings across the continent.

The problem was that there was a rumour some people had been invested with a terrible power.

It was said that when a man shook hands with one of these people, his penis would disappear. If a woman was the unlucky victim, her nipples would invert.

double *your money*

Another epidemic of rumour across west Africa concerned a mysterious stranger. The traveller would appear on the outskirts of a village, and collar one man.

He'd claim he was a marabou, or sorceror, and tell the villager that if he put his money into a magic wooden box, the cash would be doubled.

If he was stupid or superstitious – or both – the villager might put his wedge into the box. The stranger would disappear behind a big baobab tree, warning the man not

115

to look or evil would befall him. And when he came out again, the box would contain exactly double the amount the man put in.

As a special concession, he'd say, if the villager put his family's money in the box, the gods would double that too. The money would be doubled, and the delighted family would be amazed at their luck.

Then the sorceror would suggest – even though he'd been far too generous already – that the whole village could put their savings in the box, in order to double it.

After the usual deliberations, the villagers and chiefs would put all their life savings in the box. The stranger would disappear behind the baobab with the usual warnings not to follow him, and then not reappear for some time.

The villagers would eventually risk a peek behind the tree, and see the 'sorceror' scampering away hell-for-leather into the bush with all their cash.

hard *to swallow*

A couple from Surrey went on the holiday of a lifetime on safari in Tanzania, and did the works – snapping all the big game, cruising on Lake Victoria, and camping out under wide star-spangled tropical skies. It was a rough but exhilarating experience.

One night towards the end of their stay, the guides pitched camp in the middle of a huge game reserve. They had a marvellous meal round the campfire, and then retired to their respective tents.

But during the night, the woman awoke in the pitch black to find that the whole of one arm had gone dead.

Lifting up the side of the tent, she was horrified to see that a huge snake had swallowed her arm right up to the shoulder, and screamed out for help.

Instantly, one of the guides arrived on the scene, drew a knife and slit the beast open from top to tail.

The woman escaped with just a few bruises and an understandable dread of snakes.

kenyan *customs*

The brother of a bloke I work with recently witnessed an appalling event at an African airport.

He'd been visiting relatives in the former British colony of Kenya, and was stuck in one of the notorious customs scrums at Nairobi airport, when he spotted a famous musician in the melée.

The man, a renowned Kenyan Asian sitar player, with many top ten Asian hits to his credit, was returning from a lucrative concert tour. So he was dressed up to the nines in cream silk kurta pyjamas, and dripping with gold.

He approached the customs desk and after exchanging 'Jambos' was asked if he had anything to declare. The musician leaned forward on to the table and shook his head. The customs officer, upset at the affrontery of not being offered the traditional bribe, and spotting the sitar player's gold rings, grabbed his hand, shouting 'What is this, then?'

He tried violently to pull the jewellery off.

The rings wouldn't budge so *bosh!* – he chopped his fingers off with a machete and kept those as well.

don't *fetch!*

A bloke I know about knew someone who had a farm in Namibia before independence. It can be tough scratching a living from the African soil, so this farmer decided to diversify, and stocked his irrigation dam with fish.

For a while everything went swimmingly. The farmer enjoyed a diet of fried fish, baked fish, coddled fish – it was fish with everything, and what he couldn't eat he sold at the market for a pretty penny.

The fish multiplied at such a rate they made rabbits look celibate, and soon there were more fish than you could shake a stick at – far too many to catch, and when they started to clog up the sluices and irrigation system, the farmer knew something had to be done.

He happened to mention the problem to a soldier who was billeted nearby to guard the white-owned farms from attack. The squaddy thought he could help. 'Dynamite's the only answer,' he concluded. 'I'll be round at the weekend and we'll blow the bloody things out of the water.'

That weekend, standing at the edge of the dam, the soldier handed a lighted stick of dynamite to the farmer, generously suggesting that as it was his farm, he should have the honour of the first throw. The farmer arched back and hurled the explosive far out into the dam.

But out of sheer habit his faithful labrador leapt straight into the water and retrieved the fizzing explosive, swimming back to the shore.

The blokes ran like billy-o with the hapless hound closing fast, until the dynamite blew, demolishing a nearby chicken shed along with Fido.

Fish feature in another story that appeared in the *Guardian* (down the line from Reuters) in November 1992, and which has all the traits of an apocryphal-tale-turned-news-story. If this isn't an urban myth, it should be: 'An amateur angler choked to death on a live fish, Thai newspapers reported yesterday. Nakorn Hawthong was holding a fish he had caught in his teeth because he did not have a basket, but the fish became lodged in his throat.'

express *yourself*

Deep in darkest Siberia a Russian spoonbender-type was earning a small entrepreneurial fortune in the newly capitalist Commonwealth of Independent States, with amazing displays of his mental power.

The Rasputin-esque performer proved his mastery of mind over matter with spoon-bending, telekinesis of small objects and clock stopping, and had developed something of a following. But all this was in mere preparation for the big one: halting a speeding express train.

Tickets were sold for the event, and at dusk a large crowd assembled at the allotted spot on the Trans-Siberian railway. Dressed in full Cossack apparel, the mentalist waited for the heavy rumble of an approaching train, climbed the embankment and planted his feet well apart within the whistling rails.

Putting his fingers to his temples, he bowed his tousled head slightly and glowered malevolently down the glistening track with his steely grey eyes.

As the huge engine hurtled into view, its headlight blazing, the mesmerist focused the full force of his mental energy – and was promptly splattered by the thundering black express.

a grizzly *experience*

A girlfriend of my girlfriend's went off on holiday with a couple of her crazy mates. They booked a last-minute package deal from a cheap and cheerful bucket shop: two weeks in Turkey, Club Fez, £115.99 each – can't be bad.

Things were looking good, it was scorching when they touched down, and they'd already been chatted up twice just waiting for the bus.

But after the first few days of sun 'n' fun the tanned trio were getting fed up with the attentions of sozzled lager louts from Birkenhead and decided to seek out some local talent. Catching a bus inland to a nearby village, the three wandered around the dusty streets before settling down in a town square bar.

As the evening drew in, crowds of people began to gather, a huge fire flickered to life and the band struck up. Intoxicating rhythms danced on the breeze as the lasses hammered back the local grape in the twilight. Then two dreamboat locals, swarthy fellows sporting Zapata moustaches with their magnificent dark eyes sparkling, swept the young woman's two mates off to dance.

As she watched her chums being whirled round by the athletic Turkish hunks, another bottle arrived and the woman downed it quickly – still no one had asked her to dance. Buoyant with alcohol, she decided to take matters into her own hands and left the verandah for the pulsating crowd. Feeling a bit squiffy, she pushed her way into the centre of the heaving mass of writhing bodies.

And then their eyes met. She felt his heavy hands on her shoulders. He was big and hirsute with lovely brown eyes. The language barrier was no impediment, they hugged close, swaying to the exotic rhythm. He groaned erotically in her ear and licked her face in passion. Her head was still in a romantic whirl, when after a couple of clinches the crowd thinned and the stranger left her, lumbering off into the shadows without a word. Heartbroken, the young

Brit stumbled back to the bar and fell asleep on one of the tables.

She woke in the morning with a splitting headache. Remembering a little of the previous night's events, she beckoned to the bartender clearing away glasses, and begged to know who was the tall dark gentleman she had been dancing with.

'Man? What man?' he replied. 'The last time I saw you, madam, you were cavorting with the local dancing bear.'

heaven *scent*

My friend's French evening-class teacher heard an interesting story from a friend of hers who's an air hostess for Air France.

A glamorous fortysomething woman – you know the type, all diaphanous chiffon scarves, pink poodles and 'Dahlink'-ing everyone – was travelling from Paris to New York. She was a regular air traveller and as usual had the nerve to browbeat the aircrew into giving her an upgrade from economy to first class. She felt far more at home sitting nearer the front amongst people of breeding, and pestered the staff for all those little extras the blue-bloods of society come to expect: complimentary cushions, free cocktails and executive paper slippers, that sort of thing.

Apparently, an hour or so into the flight, the woman laid her heart-shaped box of chocs on the seat and visited the first-class convenience.

After powdering her nose in the tiny cubicle, she couldn't help but drench herself with a large bottle of perfume she'd picked up cheap in the duty free. She really overdid it, spraying on gallons of the stuff: behind the ears, wrists, cleavage, ankles, the lot.

Then as she left the closet, she popped a fresh king-size cigarette into her long lacquered holder and flicked open her Zippo. But to the horror of other passengers and crew, the cheap cologne ignited and she was engulfed from head to toe in a ball of flame.

wang *end of the stick*

A high-flying executive friend who works for a huge Japanese multinational was enjoying his first visit to the heart of the beast in Tokyo.

One day, he was taken on a tour of the shopping centres, to be shown how Japanese electronics stores' displays compare to those in their UK counterparts.

It was December, but mindful that most Japanese are Shinto and not Christian, the foreign guest was surprised to see that the windows were full of glitzy Christmas themes and tender nativity scenes.

His Japanese guide explained that the shops there use any old festive occasion in order to increase sales, adding that in a few months the stores would be full of Chinese New Year ephemera.

Somehow, though, in one department store, the window dressers hadn't quite got the story right. In an exotic display, the tourist was treated to the sight of Santa Claus in all his glory – nailed to a cross.

mythellaneous

Foreign

✱ Russian tankers are nearly always fitted with false bottoms these days, to dupe their trading partners

✱ American plane seats are built wider than European ones

✱ Sri Lankan motorcyclists wear their jackets inside out

✱ 80 per cent of American schoolchildren can't throw a ball

✱ In a recent crash between two motorbikes in India, involving no other vehicles, seventeen people were injured

✱ According to Texan history books, Napoleon won the battle of Waterloo

✱ There's a hotel in Phoenix, Arizona where the carpet clashes with the other well-considered decor. It's a muddy, red-brown pattern designed to hide the scorpions that crawl in from the desert

✱ The latest fad in the Far East is cow-dung sniffing. Police are trying to stamp it out

✱ Another craze in Thailand involves fermenting cabbage for liquor in barrels on roofs. Often the oriental sun proves too hot and the vats explode, demolishing the building

✱ Roman soldiers used to keep any spare change in their mouths so the enemy wouldn't hear them coming

friends *and relations*

Nowt so queer as folk

From the cradle to the grave there are myths for every milestone on the highway of life: even if you survive your young brother throwing you out of the window, the ropey rituals of a rocky marriage, and the best intentions of your mates, you've still got the perils of old age to look forward to – and dread.

phone *home*

A double-glazing salesman in south London was ringing a contact telephone number he'd been given, and the receiver was picked up immediately at the other end. A tiny voice whispered:

'Hallo?'

'Hallo, can I speak to your daddy please?' said the caller.

'No, he's busy,' replied the little voice.

'Your mummy, then. I'll speak to her.'

'You can't. She's busy too.'

'Is there anyone else there?' persisted the caller.

'Yes,' the voice conceded, 'a policeman, but he's busy as well.'

'Anyone else?' The caller was now getting a little exasperated.

'Yes, a social worker.'

'Well, can I speak to the social worker, then?'

'No, she's busy too,' said the soft little voice.

'Look, you've got all those people at your house and they're all busy. What are they *doing*?' asked the caller.

'Looking for me,' came the whispered reply.

taking *the Michael*

A woman who used to go to my uncle's fish shop in one of the less salubrious parts of Liverpool was bringing up two kids in a cramped flat on the second floor of a tenement block.

The children were Dave – he was four-and-three-quarter years old – and Mike, who was a baby.

One summer's day, the woman had to zip out briefly to the shops, and she left the two nippers on their own as usual. But as she crossed the brown grassy area at the front of the block, she suddenly realised that she'd forgotten her front door key, and as Davey wasn't yet tall enough to reach the door-lock, she feared she'd be locked out and her kids locked in.

So she stopped and hollered above the traffic noise to their open window, 'Davey, Davey,' until her eldest's head appeared through the net curtain.

'Get my key and throw it out the window, Davey lad.'

But her son couldn't quite understand her and bawled back, 'Wha'?'

'Throw my key out of the window.'

Even more bewildered, the lad asked her if she was sure. 'Of course, throw my key out of the window.'

Unfortunately, her obedient son followed her instructions – and hurled his young brother Mikey out into the wild blue yonder.

> A slight misunderstanding of a name can lead to all sorts of difficulties and embarrassments: take the apocryphal person who goes into a garden centre and asks for a 'clitoris plant'; or the young woman at the doctor's with a bad back: asked by the quack how she sleeps, she replies 'in the coital position'.

six *education*

The sister of a bloke at work, a mother with a six-year-old daughter, was alarmed one day when she asked her treasure what she'd learned at school that day.

'Oh, Miss has got us into sex at the moment,' said the precocious little girl.

Her mother looked at her agape in astonishment. She was all in favour of openness and sex education, but this seemed a bit premature, not to mention sinister.

'What did you say – "into sex"?' ventured the worried mother, on the point of ringing the headmistress to complain.

'Yes, mummy. You know: spiders, beetles – intersects.'

naïvety *play*

The friends of a family we know have a precocious eight-year-old who counted as his girlfriend a little girl who attended the same school.

During the Christmas term, the kids were selected for parts in the traditional nativity play. The boy was extremely upset at the casting: his girlfriend landed the part of Mary, but he didn't get to play Joseph opposite her. Nevertheless he took his role seriously and all the rehearsals went smoothly.

Come the big night, all the parents were glowing with pride as they watched the heart-warming performance. Cushion-pregnant Mary and her carpenter husband Joseph duly arrived at the inn with their wooden horse and asked if there was a room for the night.

It was the little boy's big moment, and he didn't disappoint.

"Course you can, Mary,' he shouted, grabbing her by the arm, 'but Joseph can sod off!'

> Apparently, later in the same play, Mary was tending to the little doll, new-born in the manger, when one of the shepherds haltingly asked what she was going to call the infant. Mary dried for a minute, thinking hard. Then her face lit up, and she replied, 'Julia'.

a Harrowing *event*

A friend of a friend attended a 'famous name' educational establishment in the late sixties. The place was renowned for the severity of its discipline, and the headmaster was unafraid to use the cane. In fact he used it whenever possible and often during school hours. (When none of the boys had misbehaved, he'd turn the stick on himself – just to keep in practice.)

The sons of the privileged were subjected to a constant diet of corporal punishment, verbal abuse and unabated bullying from Wacko and his staff.

Eventually, the boys could take no more, and in a spontaneous uprising threw off the shackles of oppression. They bound and gagged the headmaster (who seemed rather to enjoy it), imprisoned the staff in one room, and in a renunciation of all the school stood for, ran the red flag up the school flagpole.

> The incident was of course hushed up and the ringleaders packed off to Eton, while the headmaster quit to spend more time with his family. How many of the boys might today be captains of industry? And how many people retelling this story have seen the film *If?*

passing *out*

A mate from Preston was taking his GCSEs at the local comprehensive. One particular lad in their class, a bit of a swot, was swaggeringly confident about his grades right up until a few weeks before sitting – after that, the nearer the day of reckoning drew, the clammier his palms became.

When the first day of examinations actually dawned, the lad was quaking in his boots. The reluctant fifth-formers trooped into the dusty hall, checking the notes on their sleeve cuffs hadn't smudged, and set about strewing biros, assorted gonks, Snoopys and sundry lucky mascots about their desks.

The worried lad squirmed in his seat, flushed hot and cold, and began shaking slightly. When the examiner asked them to turn over their papers and begin the poor boy's head was swimming. He glanced at the questions, then panicked.

He put two sharpened pencils up his nose, leant back and smashed his head forward on to the desk, which drove the pencils up into his brain and killed him instantly.

Needless to say the other shocked candidates suffered an even worse fate – they had to sit the exam all over again at a later date. Another quick, questionable myth:

bubble *trouble*

A cheeky pupil, hopeless at maths, writes all the important formulae down on a sheet of paper which he keeps on his knees during the O-level exam. The invigilator hears rustling, suspects foul play, and correctly detects the perpetrator. So she asks the pupil to stand up, expecting the crib-sheet to fall to the floor (as does the pupil).

But when the pupil rises, no paper falls into view. The teacher is apologetic and embarrassed; the pupil is puzzled but greatly relieved. He reaches under the desk for the crib-sheet, and finds that some freshly stuck bubble-gum had kept the paper out of sight.

a friend *of the family*

A guy at work commutes to the office in west London by express coach. For years he shared the journey every day with two other blokes from the same village in Dorset, and the three of them would sit together and jaw all the way to reduce the boredom.

Then for a few months the guy was working elsewhere and didn't travel up to London.

When he next had to commute to the Big Smoke by coach, he was quite surprised to see the two old friends sitting apart; one at the front, one at the back.

He only really liked one of them, so nodding to the other, made his way to the back. Naturally, he asked why the mates were avoiding each other.

The bloke sighed, and related his story – he was a broken man. Apparently, some time ago the other commuter, Fred, had split up with his wife, and, feeling sorry for him, the storyteller, Sid, had invited him around for dinner. They'd had a great night, but Sid got a little concerned when his sixteen-year-old daughter appeared subsequently to have a crush on his mate, always asking after him and when he was coming round again. A little later she began mysteriously disappearing in the evenings and avoiding her parents' questions about where she was going.

On his daughter's seventeenth birthday, a few weeks later, Sid arranged a surprise slap-up dinner for her, but was dismayed to hear she'd already arranged a date.

'Who with?' he demanded. After a little sheepish stalling, the young belle admitted it was Fred. The ensuing confrontation ended in tears.

Incensed, Sid rang up his old pal to put things straight.

'Look,' he pleaded, 'you're old enough to be her grandad. Please, leave her alone before you break up my family.'

A few weeks later, ferreting around his daughter's room, Sid came across a love letter – from the dreaded Fred – which read, 'I spoke with your dad last night, and he told me to leave you alone, but I still want to keep our dates as usual, and I'm glad you do too.'

The two friends had a showdown the next day in the scene of so many happy times, the coach. They sat down next to each other.

'Look me old mate,' Sid began, 'this is breaking up the family, it's coming between me and you, and it's not doing anyone any good. It's got to stop.'

'Which one?' said Fred, 'your daughter or your wife?'

left *baggage*

One evening a Norwegian friend of someone at the squash club was driving with his wife from one end of the main north–south motorway to the other.

As anyone who's been to the land of the fjords will tell you, the country may not be very wide but it is very long, so deep into the night he was still driving.

Bored and tired, he resolved to have a pit-stop, recharge the batteries and empty his bladder at one of the many service stations. This he did, leaving his slumbering spouse in the passenger seat.

Suitably refreshed and relieved, he got back into the car, tuned the radio into a station that was playing some nice toe-tapping mellow music and roared away.

It was some hundred miles later that he realised things were rather quiet – then noticed to his consternation that his wife was no longer sitting in the passenger seat.

She'd obviously answered the call of nature back at the same service station; the problem was he was so weary, no matter how hard he tried, he couldn't for the life of him recall which service station he'd stopped at.

> No prizes for guessing the inevitable variations on that left-luggage theme: how about the sleeping baby absent-mindedly abandoned in a supermarket shopping trolley, for starters? As this next chilling tale indicates, you should never leave your babe among strangers . . .

134

a trip *out*

A young couple from Totnes had barely been out since the birth of their seven-month-old baby, and were frantic to get out more, especially as they were missing out on lots of Christmas parties.

In desperation the wife asked a friend if her teenage daughter might like to look after the baby while they went out on Christmas Eve. The woman said that her daughter had other plans, but if she could bring her boyfriend as well, she'd probably agree to babysit.

When the pair arrived on the 24th, the parents were a bit concerned at the grungy appearance of the boy, who looked like a druggy new age traveller. But they were so happy to be going out they put their fears aside, and had a great night out.

At the end of the evening, the couple returned home to an unfamiliar smell – perhaps it was the whiff of a takeaway the babysitters had had. The mother traced it to the kitchen while her husband went to thank the teenagers. Sadly, he found the pair spaced-out and obviously under the influence of some hallucinatory drugs.

The girl was totally out of it. But the boy managed to slur something about stuffing the turkey for them. Just then the wife let out an ear-splitting shriek from the kitchen – the childminders had roasted their poor baby by mistake.

home *and away*

An impressionable young woman working for a London PR firm met the man of her dreams at a press launch. He was so smooth-talking, so sincere and kind, so funny too, that she was swept off her feet and didn't really notice that she was being plied with drinks.

He seemed a well-to-do sort of bloke, with a motor to match his mouth, and the woman allowed herself to be driven home by him in his flash car after he'd filled her mind with all sorts of glamorous stories about his playboy lifestyle. Not wishing to appear unworldly, and feeling more than a little tipsy, the lass found herself not protesting when he said he was taking her back to his place.

Half-dazed by the champagne and this whirlwind suitor, before she knew it the young woman was hanging on his arm as they walked briskly along the dark road to his house. It seemed an unusually quiet street, but she'd guessed he lived in a select neighbourhood. He fumbled for his key – she vaguely remembered thinking it was quite sweet that he was nervous too – and then hissed 'Don't turn on the lights, it's more romantic in the dark.' The couple's frenzied passion knew no bounds. Their discarded clothes marked a tangled trail to the master bedroom.

The next morning the young woman was woken by the sound of embarrassed voices – there was no trace of her moonlight lover. But gathered at the end of the bed were a red-faced estate agent and a handful of prospective buyers shuffling uncomfortably.

All became horribly clear when the young woman spotted a big sandwich-board sign just outside the window that read 'Executive Show Home – View By Appointment Only'.

kitty *go home*

A young woman from Coventry was meeting her fiancé's parents for the first time and arrived a little late but was greeted with genuine warmth by her prospective parents-in-law.

After some initial awkwardness, the conversation flowed as smoothly as the wine, and everything was going swimmingly. Until, that is, the family tom cat, which had been eyeing her up all evening, jumped up, claws out, into her lap.

The poor guest was startled out of her skin and jumped up shrieking, sending the table and all its contents flying.

Unhappily, an argument then ensued about the pussy: the young woman, all of a lather, explained in feverish terms how much she hated cats and that she was actually allergic to them. The parents and her fiancé, devoted to their cherished family pet, dismissed her attitude as wholly unreasonable.

Eventually, the row was resolved, but a simmering tension remained between her and the family when they retired to their separate beds.

That night the young woman had a nasty nightmare in which the same wretched moggy attacked her by jumping on her chest and trying to scratch and bite her neck. She woke up extremely agitated, but soon worked out that nothing was amiss and there was no sign of the cat. Relieved, she thought no more of it and fell back to her slumbers.

In the morning, she put everything down to a bad dream after too much red wine and Stilton and wandered into the en suite bathroom. When she looked in the mirror, though, she was horrified to see scratches and claw marks all over her neck and chest – clearly not the work of a human hand.

Without further ado, she dressed, packed her stuff and left, never to see the fiancé again.

> Weddings, with so much research material to offer students of Sod's Law, are one of the most fertile areas for urban mythology. The next selection suggests that when you tie the knot, you should make sure it's double . . .

a smashing *honeymoon*

The brother of a bloke I work with planned a lovely summer wedding to his childhood sweetheart.

A plumber by trade, he was a bit worried about any pranks that his mates might play – especially after the wicked stag night, where he'd been stripped naked, covered in boot polish and handcuffed onto the night train to Inverness.

But the wedding went off blissfully and after 'Birdy Song'-ing the night away they slipped off to their elegant country-house hotel retreat for the wedding night nuptials.

The car was decked out with the predictable balloons and shaving foam, but the groom was still worried; things were going all too smoothly.

The couple checked in and were led up to the honeymoon suite. The groom was still nervous and insisted on checking the room for hidden microphones – it would be just like his mates to bug the room.

It was the bride that found it – an oversize bolt head, badly concealed under one of the big Indian rugs.

The vindicated groom scuttled down to the car and returned with his tool kit. The couple were finishing screwing the large bolt out of the floor when it suddenly went loose.

Moments later they heard a deafening, shattering crash, as a priceless antique chandelier fell from below them and smashed into smithereens on the lobby's hard marble floor.

last *night*

Some local lads were having a stag night and had been out on the town since opening time that morning.

The revelry continued all day and into the night until eventually the groom (whose drinks were severely spiked from the off) lapsed into a state of alcoholic oblivion.

He was so drunk he wasn't even able to grope the strippagram his mates had laid on specially, so they happily did the honours for him. In the early hours they were thrown out of the club and dragged the groom back towards his house across the park.

Then one bright spark decided to nick a rowing boat, and things rapidly degenerated. The drunken crew struck out for a lonely island in the middle of the municipal lake, and dumped the unconscious groom on the muddy islet.

They all thought it was a brilliant laugh to leave the

insensible groom there overnight – that was, until the next day, when he was found washed up on the shore, drowned.

five-*year hitch*

Some friends of our vicar, a perfect, lovey-dovey couple, had lavishly celebrated their fifth wedding anniversary.

Then one day the wife caught her hubby whispering furtively into the telephone. He slammed the receiver down as soon as he saw her, but couldn't conceal his embarrassment.

The couple had a blazing stand-up row, with the wife accusing her husband outright of having a covert affair. The flustered geezer blew his top, refuted the accusation vehemently and slammed the door behind him as he stormed off to the pub.

Blubbing into her hanky, the cunning spouse carefully lifted the receiver on their modern telephone and pressed the last number redial button.

A tearful woman's voice answered at the other end. Her worst fears confirmed, the wife blurted out, 'You rotten cow, how could you steal my man away from me? We've been happily married for five years.'

The other woman retorted, 'Never mind that! How d'you think I feel? The swine's just finished with me after seven years!'

> The following story is a happening new myth –
> a new entry on the myth parade, if you like –
> and a new twist on the 'almost perfect wedding'
> story.

near *the knuckle*

A friend's best mate from back home in the country was getting married in September.

The dresses had been made: a lovely cream satin, figure-hugging, off-the-shoulder number for the blushing bride, and an uncomfortable pink nylon princess-line for the bridesmaid.

The bride had been planning the marriage ceremony with military precision throughout her two-year engagement and chose a summer wedding to show off her English rose complexion and tumbling Jane Seymour-like tresses to their best advantage in the photographs.

As the big day approached, the bride-to-be began taking long, Brontë-esque walks down by the sun-flecked river in the long summer afternoons.

On one such day, she was meandering through a field back to the village when she heard something behind her. Just in time, she turned to see a fearsome, snorting bull charging headlong towards her, and she ran full pelt for the safety of a remote gate.

She could feel the beast's beefy breath on her neck, and vaulted desperately to clear the rickety five-bar gate.

But her large engagement ring snagged on a rusty nail, and although she made it to safety, her wedding finger was yanked off and left on the gate.

Here are two stories indirectly linked by the perils of hire purchase, the never-never, or extended credit – which is exactly what you'll require to believe these.

141

take *a chance*

A woman who had been dutifully and hopefully filling out her pools coupon for more years than she cared to remember was amazed one Sunday morning to see in her paper that she was at last amongst the winners with the maximum 24 points. She exploded with joy and straight away told her equally exhilarated four-year-old son and her husband, who gazed heavenward and looked like the cat that got the cream.

On the Monday, the husband went to work as usual, his head buzzing with the prospect of all that loot. But they didn't know how much they were due, and his wife had said she'd ring up the pools company to check as soon as the office opened. At lunchtime, the husband expectantly rang home to hear the result. His son answered, saying Mum had had to nip next door for a minute.

'D'you know how much money she's won, son?' asked Dad.

'Yeh, about £66,000,' chirruped Son.

After that, wild horses couldn't have halted the bloke as he rushed out of the office and drove straight to a car showroom where he'd seen a smart peacock blue Escort XR3i with soft top. Sure enough the motor was still there, and the bloke negotiated an HP deal and a trade-in for his old banger. Then he rushed and drew out his life savings in lieu of his wife's forthcoming wedge, and that evening he drew up outside their terraced house smoking a big Cuban cigar and honking his horn in the spanking new four-wheeler.

His wife stepped outside and, smiling cautiously, asked where he'd got the money from to buy it.

'Well, it can come out of your pools winnings, can't it?'

'But I rang to check, and they said I'd only won £1.60,' said his wife.

The bloke looked distraught – all his life savings up in smoke. He stammered, 'But when I rang up earlier Jimmy said you'd won £66,000.'

'Oh my God – he was talking about our Monopoly game.'

privatised *depression*

A social worker mate in Glasgow had to visit a woman who's been put through the mill due to the incompetent Tories' recession. The worst slump since the 1930s had decimated her life. Nothing was going right.

The company she worked for had sacked her and then gone bust, so she'd had no redundancy money after sixteen years' service. Her husband had lost his well-paid job in the building trade and they'd fallen way behind on their mortgage.

The house was about to be repossessed, but it had plummeted in value so they owed the building society more than it was worth. The car and all the furniture on HP had been taken by the bailiffs, and every letter was a final demand.

Finally, the strain of living on the breadline had wrecked their marriage and her husband had left to build a new life for himself down south. It was the last straw; the poor woman had had enough, and decided to end it all. So she opened the oven, stuck her head inside and switched the gas full on.

But she woke the next day with a stinking headache, to find the gas supply had been cut off.

paper*boy*

A husband from Peckham, who'd spent too much time on his work and felt he'd been neglecting his wife, one day resolved to turn over a new leaf and do right by his missus.

So early the next morning he told his surprised wife to have a lie-in – he'd collect the paper and fetch her breakfast in bed.

Feeling good about himself, the bloke heard the paper-boy approaching and collected the paper, but as he turned away from the letter box, he felt a cold hand goose his bare backside.

Furiously, he opened the door and rattled off some choice words to make quite sure the over-sexed teenager never reached in and groped his wife again.

Neighbouring curtains twitched, but he didn't care who heard him.

Then he noticed his cold-nosed labrador standing next to him, and realised he'd stupidly mistaken its affectionate greeting for the paperboy's.

give *him the boot*

Some friends met a middle-aged woman from Bexley on holiday in Greece on her own. After several jaunty days and evenings spent together, she seemed eager to get some-thing off her chest and confided in them.

She explained that she'd been married for 30 years, but

in recent years the children had left home, she was going through 'the change', and to top the lot, in recent weeks she feared her husband was having an affair – he'd started having regular baths, coordinating his shirt, tie and sock colours, eating with his mouth closed – that sort of thing.

Eventually, she caught him out when she rang the hotel room he said he was staying in on a business trip, and at midnight his secretary answered.

When he got home unaware that his wife knew about his dalliance, the husband was greeted by a scene straight out of *Misery* – his wife lunged at him with a carving knife, and succeeded in stabbing him to death in a frenzy of emotional torment.

With the help of proprietary cleaning fluids she was able to get the blood out of the hall carpet, but couldn't think what to do with the body of her philandering spouse.

In the end, she wrapped in it bin-bags, put it in the boot of her car and set off for the local hardware shop to buy the standard body-disposal tackle: rope, saw, acid etc.

But when she emerged from the store, she was horrified: the car had been stolen, and with it her husband's body.

Revenge is sweet, but doesn't always smell so . . .

pole-*axed*

A friend whose girlfriend caught him *in flagrante* in bed with another woman came home to find his live-in lover had quietly but unsurprisingly flown the nest.

For a few weeks he revelled in his new bachelor status, then invited his new lady to share the flat. After a few weeks of freedom the apartment looked awfully untidy and a pungent pong had taken root in the bedroom.

Apparently, the jilted girlfriend had stuffed an economy packet of party prawns inside the curtain poles. No matter what they tried – the great smell of Brutal, disinfectant everywhere, joss sticks, changing his socks – the nostril-attacking niff remained, worsening by the week.

Over the summer months, the whiff had graduated from a honk to a genuine hum, and very fishy it was too.

In fact the smell got so bad that after changing all the furniture the couple decided to move out. The endemic stench meant they were forced to accept a price for the flat far below market value, but they were happy to be leaving the pong behind.

It just so happened that the former girlfriend got wind they were moving out and was passing as they were packing the van.

With great pleasure, she watched the removal men take down the brass curtain poles and carry them into the van bound for the new apartment.

There are many other vengeful stories of this ilk, often associated with jilted lovers. One tale has the spiteful former paramour sowing water cress in a carpet (most entertainingly in the bathroom carpet, where a fresh crop appeared after every shower). Another story concerns two lads with a rudimentary knowledge of motors but a master's degree in mischief, who put a rotten fish in the ventilation system of their mate's car. After a few days, epecially when the engine warmed up, the whiff got pretty bad, and the poor bloke shampooed his carpet, bought Feu Orange and everything (he was convinced it was something his friend's dog had left in there), to no avail. The funniest part was, until his mates broke the news, he was turning the ventilation on full to try and purge the pong, which of course only served to make things that little bit worse.

a last *wish*

A friend's grandad lived in rural Ireland and some years ago he was enjoying one of his regular country strolls down a long straight unmade track.

As he pottered along, he noticed ahead of him a dark-looking fellow sauntering in the middle of the narrow lane. Then he heard the grind and clatter of a coach and horses approaching from behind apace.

The wandering fellow in front seemed oblivious to the noise and the old man began shouting to him to warn him of the danger, but there was no response.

So the sprightly old man started to run up to the stranger and, drawing level with him, managed to drag him to the side seconds before the speeding coach thundered by.

The dark-skinned stranger instantly came to, as if from a trance, and grabbed the old fellow.

'Jeez, old man,' he said powerfully, his deep dark eyes staring intently, 'you saved my life! Daydreaming will be the death of me.' And he insisted that his saviour share a drink with him at a nearby inn.

The stranger evaded all questions about himself, refusing

to divulge his name or purpose for being in the area, but he asked the old fellow something in return.

The first drink glowing in their stomachs, the newcomer leaned forward with gravity and posed his companion a weighty question: 'If it were possible to have *one* wish granted, what would be your desire?' And with that he went to the bar to fetch another round.

The old man pondered. He had no great need of wealth as he was financially secure; his health was just dandy; and as his friends always ribbed him for being a clever dick, he felt no need of wisdom. The obvious three eliminated, when the stranger returned to his seat, the old fellow said simply, 'If I had one wish, as you put it, it would be to stay exactly as I am. I should like to remain a healthy 58-year-old.'

The stranger looked puzzled, picked up his hat and left in a hurry.

The old fellow returned home and told his wife the whole curious story, including his wish to remain the same as he was.

The next morning his wife was left to wonder whether the stranger had indeed granted her husband's wish – as that night he'd died peacefully in his sleep.

all *is not rosy*

This friend of my grandad's was a keen but pernickety gardener – in fact, his little patch of earth (actually about a third of an acre) would have had Percy Thrower reaching for the paraquat, it was so perfect.

The National Trust coach tours detoured to pass his plot,

and he swept the board of prizes every year at the village flower show. All except his lawn, which didn't make the grade at all. So he stripped off the turf, trucked in the best top soil, then levelled and landscaped the ground. As luck would have it, he spotted a big local seed merchant was advertising cheap seeds. He rang them up and was told to come by because they needed a sample of his soil to check its chemical balance in order to select the perfect seeds. This was duly supplied. The seed merchant said they'd do the tests and ring him up. Two weeks later the lab report came in and the ideal marriage of soil and seed was planned.

The bulk seeds were delivered the next day, along with the treatments, fertilisers and bird netting essential for rapid growth. The green-fingered fellow read the instructions very carefully, did everything by the book, and sat back to watch his dream lawn emerge.

But days passed and the soil remained barren. A week, two weeks passed. Still the lawn showed not a sausage – or even a blade of grass – despite his tender loving care.

Then one night three weeks later after the sowing there was a heavy storm. The bloke woke up bleary-eyed and looked forlornly out of his bedroom window as usual – to his joy there was a sea of green all over the back garden. At last, he thought, and rushed downstairs, putting on his glasses as he went.

He burst outside into the garden and rushed over to admire the lush, verdant lawn . . . of lettuces.

you *can't keep a good man down*

A few years ago in Ireland a couple of brothers were on their way to visit their elderly grandfather a few miles outside Cork.

He was a game old gent but very advanced in years and lived all on his own. The lads arrived at the cottage and knocked loudly on the door. There was no answer, but they weren't unduly worried – the old goat was as deaf as a post.

But when they eventually pushed open the door, they found their grandfather had passed away, sitting by the fire in his favourite armchair. Due to rigor mortis, he was now as stiff as a board.

The funeral arrangements were duly made and a wake organised in the old fella's honour.

The only problem was that as he'd died in a seated position they couldn't get him to lie flat in the coffin. They had to pass a rope round his chest and legs and tie it tight under the table.

Thus fastened in a more seemly pose, they lay him in state for people to pay their last respects.

The wake was a corker: food a-plenty, gallons of drink and a good crack. The whole family turned out, all crammed in the old bloke's tiny front room.

Toast after toast was drunk to the old boy's memory and the party was going great guns until, for a laugh, one of the drunken brothers slipped under the table and cut the rope.

You've never seen a room clear so quick as when the old man's corpse suddenly sprang bolt upright.

robin *red-face*

A young Irish couple who'd been courting for some months went out for a romantic evening topped off by a visit to the pictures to see the blockbuster movie *Robin Hood – Prince of Thieves*, the all-action historical romance starring Kevin Costner.

It was a touching film, very tender, and the devoted couple especially loved the smoochy theme song, 'Everything I Do, I Do It For You', crooned by Bryan Adams. Later the same night, as they listened to 'their' song in a local pub, the boyfriend went down on one knee and proposed. His paramour enthusiastically said yes.

Come the day of the wedding the groom, waiting for

his future wife to arrive at the church, had a word with the church organist.

He asked if it was possible to break with tradition so that when the bride walked down the aisle, instead of the standard wedding march, the organist would play their song, the theme from *Robin Hood*. The organist, a stickler for convention, asked the groom if he was sure. The groom said he'd never been more sure of anything.

Minutes later, the bride's car pulled up outside. An expectant hush fell over the packed church, and as the doors opened, the organist struck up the *Robin Hood* theme as arranged.

The only problem was that the doddery old organist had never heard of Bryan Adams. So instead, he accompanied the blushing bride's ladylike procession with the jaunty and highly inappropriate 'Robin Hood, Robin Hood, riding through the glen' theme, from the hit sixties TV series of the same name.

mythellaneous

Society

�֍ The capacity at Wembley has to be reduced for rugby
league finals, because the people in the crowd are that
much fatter

�֍ Hitler only had one ball. The Russians who found his
charred body in the Berlin bunker carried out tests to
see if they could use the evidence in propaganda

✱ It's quite common for dead passengers to travel around
undisturbed for days on the Tokyo metro – even sometimes standing up

✱ The National Health Service only came into being
because during the Second World War more than half
the conscripts had rickets, polio or bad breath

✱ Dozens of commuters kill themselves on their way
home every year by falling asleep. Apparently, they
wake up confused and accidentally walk out of the
train door between stations

✱ People who live near airports often have their green-
houses smashed by frozen sewage jettisoned from planes
flying at 30,000 feet

✱ Shop mirrors are trick ones that make you look much
slimmer

✱ Lord Kitchener was a notorious china thief, and society

153

hostesses were alerted to his habit so they wouldn't kick up a stink when he lifted some porcelain

* During the war, Hitler flooded the south of England with thousands of fake £5 notes to destroy the British economy

* Don't bother separating clear bottles and coloured ones for recycling – they always mix them up again at the depot

* A headmaster who sent a sample of water from his school swimming pool for chemical analysis was surprised to receive the reply, 'This horse is very poorly and should be put down immediately.'

And finally, a few less-than-politically correct tabloid favourites:

* Humberside council insisted on political correctness for the annual Christmas pantomime, and changed the show's name to *Snow White and the Seven Vertically Challenged Persons*

* Black bin-bags and blackboards were banned by Brent council, and 'Baa Baa Black Sheep' was outlawed in Haringey junior schools, for being racist

* Islington council only gives housing and jobs to pregnant, black, Jewish, disabled lesbians

campus *capers*

Extra-curricular activities

Students! They're workshy swots who spend all their time drinking, discovering sex and drugs, and playing pranks . . . no wonder the rest of us — graduates of the School of Hard Knocks — are jealous. There's a lesson in here somewhere . . .

widen *the circle of your friends*

A bookish geography student in his second term at Lancaster University was concerned to discover one Saturday morning that his bottom was sore and aching like the aftermath of a severe vindaloo, and that his head was hurting as if he'd been on a bender all night.

Putting the experience behind him, the young freshman forgot about it until the following weekend, when he awoke with the same symptoms. In fact, this went on for weeks – every Saturday morning the quiet scholar's head was banging and his back passage burning. It began to affect his work. He was getting behind with his swotting, coming bottom in class and didn't know which way to turn, until eventually he sought advice from the campus medic. He explained the symptoms, and the doctor performed an internal examination and a blood test.

At a consultation a week later, the elderly doctor looked at the test results and at the winsome young lad, then asked him, 'Are you a practising homosexual?'

The student stammered back, 'N-no, I'm straight.'

'In that case, young man,' the doctor explained, 'you're being chloroformed and buggered every Friday night!'

pairs *of genes*

A friend who was a medical student at Manchester University and is now a GP in London wasn't always as ethically-minded as he is now.

To earn a bit on the side, and work off some of his excess energies (and other things), he became a sperm donor – test-tube babies were the new thing and the local hospital at the time offered cash for your offloaded sperm to stock their gene bank. Everyone said it was great he could earn money for what he was best at, and that it was the only bank account he'd never get overdrawn on.

Anyway, he convinced his best mate, a black student from St Lucia with even more pressing money problems, to come in on the scheme and make regular deposits for cash. The two of them would travel together holding their specimens in the back seat of a taxi so they got to the hospital within the one-hour delivery deadline for usable ejaculations.

One time, after a heavy lunchtime session, the two spunky lads were sitting in the back of the cab with their freshly-produced phials of seminal fluid, when they both started chuckling. 'Are you thinking what I'm thinking?' said one.

'Let's do it,' said the other – and they swapped their test-tubes over, leaving a racial time-bomb in the hospital's sperm bank that is probably still ticking away.

watered-*down beer*

A group of impecunious students at Leicester University was skulking in the union bar with empty glasses and even emptier pockets. The top pop group Slade were playing their hearts out at a comeback performance in the main hall so the place was packed.

The skint intellectuals were staring into their dregs, when one of them said he could stand it no more, and was going to get a pint by hook or by crook. Then he disappeared into the toilets with a pint glass. Moments later, he re-emerged from the urinal with the glass brimming and strode purposefully up to the thronging bar, notorious for its diluted beer.

Attracting the attention of a barmaid, he shouted above the clamour, 'Oi! This lager tastes like piss. I want another pint!'

The barmaid sniffed the brew, but declined to taste it, taking him at his word. Then she went to pour him another glass. Luckily, he spotted her pouring just a bit off and topping it up, and insisted he receive a fresh whole pint. So she put it to one side for a less fussy customer.

Seconds later, he was grinning like the cat that got the cream as he sauntered back to his mates, who all pronounced him a messiah for turning water into lager.

The only drink problem students have, as the antique joke goes, is not being able to afford it. Since the old common cold research centre closed down (through illness), poor students have had to resort to all sorts of money-making gambits to keep them in biros, A4 pads and baked beans.

Recently it's been reported that nearly all sections of the sex industry have been inundated with applications for work from undergraduates: gigolos, 'exotic' dancers, 0898 sex-line voice artistes – these people are our future leaders!.

plant *pot*

An agriculture student at Aston University used to travel home each summer recess to his parents' rural retreat and impress them with his enthusiasm for gardening, if not his prowess.

For each summer he'd plant a big crop of tomato plants in gro-bags in their glasshouse. But every year, the seemingly thriving plants would fail to bear fruit. The obviously disappointed son would tell his parents he'd cut them down and dispose of the cuttings, and that he'd try again next year.

One September however, the student's father happened to have a keen gardening friend, a local bobby, round for a barbecue. When the visitor was being shown round the garden, he was surprised to hear the son's horticultural attempts described as tomatoes.

'I may be very old-fashioned,' said the copper, 'but I know marijuana when I see it.'

For some reason, Mother Nature endowed the lowly tomato with a similar foliage and appearance to what Jamaicans call 'the herb that is the healing of the nation' – marijuana. (Apparently some dozy police once did a raid and were told by their chief to look out for the weed, only to ask everyone in the house if they knew where Mary Warner was, but that's another story.)

The result of this quirk is that many exploit the legitimacy of one to mask the illegality of the other. A group of students at Essex University in the seventies took to growing their own crop of tomatoes on the south-facing windowsills of their

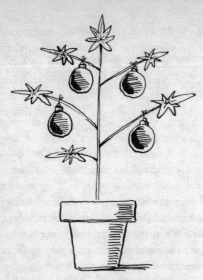

halls of residence; others grew marijuana in the same location and adorned the plants with red Christmas baubles to appear like the innocent fruits nearby.

even *pottier*

The Sheffield area isn't known as 'the Potteries' for nothing – in fact it's not known as the Potteries at all.

As you drive north on the M1 towards the steel city, the transport artery weaves between the relics of a former age: two monolithic disused cooling towers.

What to do with the huge twin white elephants is a knotty problem that has occupied the most brilliant brains in Yorkshire for the last few years. One of the smartest suggestions looks set to go ahead, and due to rank alongside Milton Keynes' concrete cows in local popularity.

Two art students in Sheffield want to paint the huge twin towers terracotta and place massive sculptures in them. So that when you drive through Sheffield in the future, you will be greeted by the world's largest flower pots containing a pair of monster daffodils.

a wee *dram*

A friend of a friend who's a student at Keele University recently went with a mate to one of those society parties at a big house in the posh part of Chelsea.

It was the daughter of the household's 21st birthday and he and some of his student mates were there on sufferance because they studied with her 'bit of rough' boyfriend.

The lads were having a brilliant time scoffing platefuls of free swanky nosh washed down with gallons of vintage bubbly. Even better, there was wall-to-wall upper-crust crumpet.

Everything went smoothly until one of the lads, a French and Woodwork student, headed for the loo, bursting. He came back relieved, but explained that the queue to the bathroom had been too long to bear and he'd had to use his ingenuity.

In the early hours, the last few guests and the family crashed out in the drawing room passing round the twelve-year-old malt whisky until the bottle was finished and the guests were politely asked to leave.

As the undergrads staggered home, one teased the French and Woodwork student that he seemed to have bottled out on the drinking front, not touching a drop of the fine old malt while the rest gave it a good hammering.

'Well,' he smirked, 'you know when I said I'd used my ingenuity . . .'

cough *up*

A mate at college in Bristol heard about a flat full of medical students who were always up to pranks.

It was basically a non-smoking household except for one young hedonist who went through fags like a Chippendale through condoms. All his flatmates hated the smell and his habit of leaving tea cups and plates of food around with dog-ends squashed on them, so they rather enjoyed it when he would have one of his coughing fits, which sometimes lasted several minutes.

'You'll cough your lungs up one day,' they'd all chorus cheerfully, and it became something of a catchphrase.

One day, they came home to find fag-ends and ash all over the washing up and found the smoker had gone out on the beer around the pubs of Clifton. When he got in, smelling like a brewer's ashtray, he was so paralytic he could hardly stand, and embarked on a massive coughing fit before collapsing in a heap.

The others carried him upstairs to bed, but had a mischievous idea.

In the morning, one of them nipped out early and bought a pound of fresh ox liver from the local butchers. Then he applied black felt pen and chilli relish to the liver and carried it upstairs to the still-unconscious smoker's bed, arraying it on the student's chest like it had just been coughed up.

An hour later, the smoker appeared downstairs at the breakfast table looking decidedly ill and green about the gills. The others kept a straight face. 'You were right about me coughing my lungs up – it's happened,' he groaned.

'Bet that was a horrible experience,' said one, prying hopefully.

'Not half as nasty as forcing them back in, though,' said the smoker.

surgical *spirit*

Clinical comical casualties

This catalogue of complaints is a hypochondriac's nightmare and a private clinic's dream. We're all fascinated to hear about other people's medical misfortunes – the more gruesome and peculiar the better. When the malady is closer to home, we're sure doctor knows best. But there's always a fear that if we put our life in their hands, they might just drop it . . .

pea *soup*

A district nurse in Sleaford, Lincolnshire, had on her regular round an elderly woman who was always griping about the quality of social service she was given.

Talk about looking a gift horse in the mouth! Nothing was good enough for her, from the type of dressing on the sores on her hips, to the places the council arranged pleasant day trips to.

But the churlish woman reserved her most withering criticism for the meat 'n' two veg supplied by the local 'meals on wheels' service.

One particular afternoon, the fresh-faced nurse arrived in particularly fine spirits, determined not to let the old biddy grind her down as usual. But as soon as she was in the door, the old grouch was whingeing on about the food she'd been served earlier.

'Look at that!' she thundered, pointing a wrinkly finger at a garden pea on the side of her plate. 'What d'you think that is?'

'Well,' said the nurse, trying to remain cheery, 'it's a pea, isn't it?'

'Is it?! *Is it??!!*' said the woman, even louder. 'A bullet more like. Just you feel it!'

The nurse walked over and gently squeezed the minuscule green vegetable. The old woman was right, it seemed rock hard.

'There! Just you try and chew it, see what I've to put up with,' ordered the old mare. So the district nurse picked up the pea again, warily placing it inside her mouth and bringing her jaws to bear on it.

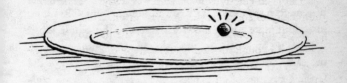

With a 'ping' the pea shot out of her mouth and bounced around the room and off the china horse collection.

'See!' barked the old woman. 'And it's been through me too!'

There are distant echoes of another carers' legend, featured in our first book of myths, about the old fellow who offers his social worker some nuts. While she's eating them, he confesses he doesn't like them as they get stuck under his false teeth. He just sucks the chocolate off them. Why do people in the caring professions have such a jaundiced view of human life? Perhaps they're actually *anti*-social workers; or perhaps it's because they're dealing with people whose own families will have nothing to do with them . . .

special *delivery*

An ageing doctor based in Norwich was coming close to retirement age and feeling the strain but still insisted, against his concerned wife's advice, on fulfilling all his GP duties, including night call – the worst aspect of the whole job.

One night when he was on call, the phone rang in the early hours. Wearily, the wrinkly medic listened to the fevered rantings of an expectant father: 'She's having contractions! The water's everywhere! Help!'

Having heard it all before, the doc knew there was probably a long way to go before any action was needed, so he calmed the bloke down and asked for more details before he set off.

It appeared that things were not as far gone as first described, so the GP suggested the prospective dad ring the midwife a little later.

An hour later, the bloke was on the blower again, even more het up. Clearly he couldn't get it together to fetch a midwife, so the bleary-eyed doctor mumbled he'd be over directly. Ten minutes later he was driving red-eyed across town in his old Morris Minor with his trousers and ill-buttoned shirt over his stripey pyjamas.

When he arrived, he found the woman was in labour. With no midwife available at such short notice, the doctor set about the home delivery himself. Despite his tiredness and the lack of painkillers, everything went swimmingly, and the woman produced a bouncing baby girl.

An hour later, the afterbirth came out. All three looked at each other and wondered what to do with it. The couple didn't have a garden to bury it in, so they implored the pale doctor to dispose of it, wrapping it in brown paper and giving him a Marks & Spencer bag to put it in.

So the doc tottered outside into the piercing light of a new day, but he was so tired he'd left the car's lights on and the battery was dead flat, so he had to wait for a bus to take him home.

He eventually got back at seven o'clock to be greeted by his wife. He explained everything that had happened and when he came to the end he suddenly stopped and put his hand to his mouth.

'What's up darling?' asked his spouse.

'I just wonder what lost property is going to make of it,' he said, realising he'd left the M&S bag on the bus.

> That's another 'something out of context and horrible in the bag' story. And pity the poor bus driver – invariably the person who makes the discovery.

what *a drag*

A young Malaysian woman began her first night shift as a nurse in a hospice in Leeds, and after a strenuous few hours settled down for a smoke and a cuppa in the staff room.

But the other nurses all pounced on her when she lit up, making it clear in no uncertain terms that smoking was strictly prohibited in the hospice and that if she wanted to continue her life-threatening anti-social habit, she'd have to do so on the roof.

It was a freezing cold, howling winter's night, but the

poor woman's dependence on the weed was so acute she braved the elements for a quick puff.

Unfortunately just as she threw the cig down to tread on it, a gust of wind slammed the door shut, and there was no way to open it. She was stuck outside.

Other staff noticed her absence, but put it down to annoyance at being told off about smoking.

In the morning, however, the poor young woman was found by a maintenance man frozen to death – with a last gasp fag still between her lips.

floored

Just round the corner from our street in Croydon, there was recently an incident in the high street.

A bulk chemical tanker was involved in an accident with a pizza delivery moped and spilled its load all over the wide road outside the busy shopping mall.

Police were soon on the scene, and just as well, for the tanker was carrying hydrochloric acid, and it was everywhere.

The cops quickly cordoned off the large affected area and stopped any cars or people proceeding.

Unfortunately, one woman, impatient to reach the shops, left her car, dodged the cordon, and ran as fast as she could across the wet road.

Police tried in vain to grab her before it was too late, but could only watch helplessly as the acid dissolved first her shoes, then her feet and finally her ankles, before she fainted outside Bejam.

funny *feline*

A young Dunfermline woman some years ago was pregnant with her first child and spent most of her days resting in her Granny's rocking chair.

Every now and then, the family cat would jump up to sit on her lap, and Granny would tut tut.

The young woman asked her what the matter was, and Granny warned her that the more she let the cat lie down on her lap, the greater the likelihood that the baby would be born with a cat's head.

Her granddaughter laughed at such an old wives' tale, and persisted in letting the moggy nestle down on her whenever it wanted.

Granny kept trying to warn her, but the mother-to-be wouldn't listen to a word of it.

As the big day drew near, the grandmother tried one last time, scooting the cat out of the room at every opportunity. But still it found its way back to the comfort of the pregnant granddaughter's lap.

When the young woman went into labour, wise old Granny knew she would be right. And sure enough, when the baby emerged into the world . . . it was perfectly normal.

Don't ask me'ow.

from *beer to eternity*

A bloke from Staffordshire was visiting his sickly uncle in hospital. The older relative had just had a serious operation, but he was only too pleased to polish off his nephew's get well gift, a couple of cans of beer – though it was strictly against doctor's orders.

Sadly, the next day the uncle was found dead in bed.

'That's ironic,' remarked the nephew on hearing the news. 'Because the beer I took him was Long Life.'

nurse *knows best*

A friend of a friend who's a nurse heard of a colleague who had a few problems in her younger days.

As a student nurse she'd been on duty, alone, in the geriatric ward at a rambling old Victorian hospital. One night, for the first time a particularly ill patient was under her supervision.

Apparently the sister had been in to check on his condition and told her that under absolutely no circumstances must the elderly patient leave his bed. Unfortunately, straight afterwards the charge nurse arrived, examined the patient and ordered the poor student nurse to put the patient on the commode chair.

The immediate contradiction threw the inexperienced angel into a complete quandary: how could she avoid disappointing either of her superiors?

Then it came to her, and she drew the curtains for privacy. Soon after, the sister and charge nurse strode back into the ward – only to be confronted by the sight of the distraught old man's head wobbling precariously above the screens.

Ingeniously the trainee had placed the commode on top of the bed.

chomping *at the bit*

A young student nurse was on duty for the first time in the geriatric ward of our local hospital. She had been instructed to carry out a number of tasks while the old folks were in the land of nod.

One of her more onerous duties was to collect all the old folks' dentures from the glasses by their beds and give them a good scrub.

Apparently the false choppers build up a thick sticky layer of tartar and nicotine that only a sterilising scour in a proprietary cleaning fluid can shift (who'd be a nurse?).

The trainee rounded up the teeth and dunked them all in a huge bowl to soak. Then yanking on her rubber gloves she attacked the task with gusto. Soon the sparkling falsies were stacked up by the sink to dry.

In the morning the grateful old folk smiled gummily, ready to receive their spruced-up sets before breakfast. Then the nurse realised her mistake. Matron blew her top – the trainee hadn't kept the teeth in pairs or made a note of which set belonged to which patient. The poor old folk had to stand in line playing musical teeth until the correct gums and plates were reunited.

Things and people were much simpler in Elizabethan days – you'd merely find a chunk of hard wearing wood and carve your own teeth, or alternatively pay some poor people to give you theirs.

as *directed*

Our family knew the husband of a health visitor in London's East End, who had some odd stories.

One involved an old man on his wife's 'beat', a crotchety fellow suspicious, like so many of his generation, of all medical professionals and their prescriptions. Because of this fear, he often withheld information about his health problems, almost until it was too late.

On one such occasion, the health visitor saw him wince as she was about to leave, and prised out of him the fact that his bottom hurt. A quick inspection ascertained that he had a severe case of haemorrhoids. A few days later, the health visitor visited the elderly gent with some suppositories to ease his 'Chalfonts'. He huffed and puffed, but grudgingly accepted them and agreed to follow the instructions on the pack.

The next week, when she came to visit the old bloke, he was even more surly than usual. She asked him if his piles had improved. 'With those things you gave me! Course they bloody haven't,' he snapped.

She asked him if he'd followed the directions. He just scoffed. 'It said "Place in your back passage", but I don't have one, so I put them in the hall. I might as well've shoved them up me bum, for all the good they've done!'

N.B. For those who choose not to flavour their

174

speech with an East End patois: according to the lexicon of cockney rhyming slang, 'Chalfonts' is short for 'Chalfont St Giles', which of course rhymes beautifully with piles.

superglue *cock-up*

A mate who works in the local hospital casualty ward recently had to attend to a rather alarming case. The patient had been badly beaten, but it was his other predicament that had the orderlies in hysterics.

Apparently the bloke had been doing a spot of DIY, mending an old teapot's broken spout, when he was caught short and had to dash to the toilet. Sadly some spilled superglue had led to his finger and thumb becoming stuck fast to his appendage and try as he might he just couldn't free them.

So in his desperation he crept round to his next door neighbour's house hoping to use the phone to call for an ambulance. After the initial shock of being exposed to her neighbour's sticky situation, she took him inside. Not wanting to trouble the overworked NHS, and being the proud possessor of a Girl Guides first aid badge, the neighbour got down on her knees to tackle the adhesive problem.

It was at that moment that her long-distance lorry-driver husband arrived home early by chance, and, perhaps understandably, totally misread the situation, giving the glue victim a terrible hiding (with one hand still stuck fast 'downstairs').

Superglue has been around now for many a year

and we've all heard about people being glued to toilet seats and having to go to hospital to have their fingers separated, but strangely there seem to be very few full-length shaggy dog stories surrounding the marvellous product.

a strange *twist*

An overweight cigar-smoking impresario friend told me a curious thespian's yarn. A tacky variety troupe were treading the boards at The Empire in Sunderland, when one of the cast fell very ill and was rushed to a local GP.

The doctor was very concerned about the listless trouper – not at all like one of his regular patients – who was sweating profusely and cut a strange figure in his crushed velvet bolero jacket and spandex trousers slumped on the doctor's couch. Taking his pulse, the quack tried to discover what was bothering the poor fellow, but the patient remained mum. Trying another tack, he lifted the artiste's leg, asking gently, 'Does this hurt?'

The bloke shook his head.

The doctor moved the leg higher and higher, trying to measure the pain threshold, until it was infeasibly twisted behind the bloke's back. Still not a wince.

Confused, the doc asked again 'Does this hurt?'

Again the man shook his head. Despite everything the doctor tried nothing seemed to be wrong with the patient, and annoyingly he still denied even any twinges.

The medic began to get frustrated and started forcing the bloke's leg further and further, twisting and bending it to try and get some reaction, but still not a groan.

The doctor finally lost his rag, accusing the itinerant showman of putting it all on, and he threw him out of the surgery.

Sadly, the next day the contortionist died of laryngitis.

This should come as no surprise to those who remember the tragic circumstances of comedian Sid James's death onstage at the same venue. As Newcastle people are keen to point out, everyone dies at the Sunderland Empire.

getting *the point*

A friend of the family had been suffering for some time with a nagging back pain. After trying all the traditional methods of treatment to no avail, he decided to try alternative medicine and visited the local acupuncturist. The practitioner was a highly regarded but faintly mysterious old man who'd been practising in the area for years.

On the day of the appointment, the suffering patient was sitting in the waiting room looking around, feeling a little nervous. But his nerves were calmed by the Cantonese certificates of qualification, which were very impressive.

The first treatment didn't hurt at all and fixed his back pain a treat, so much so that the patient began to go regularly for relief.

As it happened, the next time he paid a visit there was an Oriental gentleman in the waiting room. The bloke got talking to him, and asked him how he thought this chap compared with the real thing – Chinese acupuncturists back home.

The inscrutable old man replied, 'He's very good indeed. The only thing that concerns me is why he has a licence to sell fish in Hong Kong harbour on his wall.'

snooker *loopy*

A group of lads from a carpet dye works in Cumbria went down for their regular Friday evening drink to the local snooker hall.

Time passed quickly as they threw back the ale between occasional visits to the table. Before long they tired of the usual game and went into 'betcha can't do this' mode.

After a series of trick shots culled from the exhibition repertoire of Ray Reardon, one big-mouthed lad showed his party-piece — wrapping his lips round the top of a pint glass.

Another lad was unimpressed and bet him he couldn't fit a snooker ball in his trap.

Not one to duck a challenge, the show-off opened his mouth especially wide and, after a moment's straining and manipulation, the ball squeezed in, glinting in the table lights.

The lads whooped and hollered in appreciation, chanting 'magic, magic' until it was time to remove the ivory ball. The hero tried to pull it out, but it wouldn't budge. There appeared no way to remove the polished sphere. It was trapped behind his teeth.

The club manager was alerted, and, concerned that a death might affect business, used a trick he'd learnt in the army.

He told the panicking bloke to stand still, clenched his

fist, then struck him sharply and accurately on the jaw. Happily, the jaw was dislocated and the ball rolled out.

> In another version, the unfortunate lad is rushed to hospital with the ball still stuck fast in his mouth. The doctors decided the only way to remove the obstruction was to pull out all his teeth.
>
> That story sounds like it must have happened somewhere, struck a curious chord and spread like wildfire, until the 'snooker ball lobster pot effect' appears to have occurred in every pool room in the land.

finger-*licking good*

A friend of the bloke who lagged our hot-water tank used to work deep in the bowels of Bart's Hospital in Clerkenwell, torching boil dressings and other medical waste in the incinerator. His job involved visiting the various wards and operating theatres, emptying bins and taking away rubbish sacks.

It was on one of his forays that he came across a consultant from the urology department instructing a white-coated bunch of fresh-faced students. The well-scrubbed gaggle of undergraduates was crowded tightly round the donnish consultant eager to soak up learning. He had a small petri dish in front of him containing a sample of urine, and was discussing testing for sugars in the body and their medical implications.

'In fact,' he enthused, 'one of the simplest tests we can

do for excess sugar in the urine is the taste test.' The students shrank back cringing, but he insisted the human tongue was capable of detecting sugar quite accurately, and to prove it he quickly dipped a finger into the yellow fluid, before popping it into his mouth and nodding vigorously.

Then he made each squirming student in turn dip a digit in the 'sample' and taste it thoroughly, before asking, 'Right then – hands up who saw me switch fingers?'

body *and soul*

An acquaintance I once met at a party recently heard a strange tale from the Emerald Isle. Apparently, if you have a limb amputated in an Irish hospital, it is carefully buried in the hospital grounds. Then when you eventually shuffle off this mortal coil, no matter how many years later, you are buried alongside it.

> It's not known what happens should you be unfortunate enough to have more than one limb amputated and buried in different parts of Ireland. Perhaps there's a limb processing centre for the recently deceased, assembling all the parts in the correct order before burial. An early reference to this practice of reassembly before burial may be hinted at in the phrase 'bury my heart at wounded knee'.

a slice *of life*

A friend who lives down in Sussex knows of an old lady nearby who recently had to go to hospital for a minor operation. Before the op, the surgeon in charge decided to give the old dear the once over, to see if there was anything else that needed fixing that he could do all in one go when she was on the slab. (Time is money in the new market NHS.)

The shy old lady wasn't keen to be examined, but reluctantly agreed. The quack gave her a thorough examination

181

and couldn't help noticing that one of the old dear's large flat breasts seemed slightly mis-shapen.

On closer examination the surgeon was shocked to uncover a cheese sandwich nestling beneath her sagging bosom.

'Oh, I wondered where that had got to,' said the old lady, hastily snatching it back.

Health

* Rainforest Indians have a cure for every disease known to man, but pharmaceutical companies sponsor gold prospectors to wipe them out so we never hear about them. If the public heard about these simple remedies, the companies would be put out of business.

* If you experience a strong sensation of smelling oranges for no reason, it means you're just about to have a brain haemorrhage

* They can repair literally anything with key-hole surgery these days

* Sit on wet grass, cold stone steps or a hot radiator, and you're bound to get piles

* A bloke who was deaf in one ear once lost his digital watch somewhere in his bedroom, and was driven mad by not being able to find it when the beep went off every hour

* When laser surgery is in progress in an operating theatre, new nurses often complain about the smell of sizzling bacon

* Have all your teeth pulled out and you'll never suffer from arthritis

* A hospital in Edinburgh had an electric shock treatment

machine fitted and reported fantastic results. When an engineer came to service it after a year, he found it hadn't been connected to the electricity

* Breasts grow to fit the size of your bra, but the breast over the heart is always bigger than the other because it gets more blood

* Everyone has a relative who's 85, has smoked and drunk all his life, and is as fit as a butcher's dog

* Whenever you've got a gynaecological problem, you're booked in with a GP of the opposite sex

xxx-rated

___

Raunchy risqué romps

Everything you really didn't want to know about sex – but were too curious to miss. Social inadequates who wouldn't normally say 'taboo' to a goose bare all and go bonking bonkers in our 'downstairs' department. Those of a nervous disposition should only read the following chapter once . . .

hold *your loved one*

A bloke at a mate's rugby club in Hereford fancied himself as something of a ladies' man, though our mate always reckoned he was all mouth and trousers. But there was one happy occasion when the trousers were all too absent.

This rugger-bugger was earning the inflated wage of an estate agent (before the nineties concept of negative equity ruined their fun), and was always out drinking, but still lived at home to save money and be waited on hand and foot by his long-suffering, salt-of-the-earth mum.

Out late one night after a bladderful with the lads, the bloke felt randy rumblings in his nether regions. So as soon as he got home, he ran two stairs at a time up to the privacy of his bedroom and turned on the telly to check if there were any late night kit-off films on the box – he didn't have a satellite for 'Red Hot Dutch', so he normally settled for lukewarm Welsh.

His pulse raced when he saw a foreign film listed in the wee small hours – with oh-so-sexy subtitles – so he kept himself awake and then flashed channels to see the EC flesh mountain unfold. As he did so, he threw his duvet on the floor and took his impetuous member in an expectant hand.

Disappointingly, the film turned out to be something of a French art-house bore, but the estate agent kept his percy stimulated, ever-hopeful of a flash of brown bits against the run of play.

However, the next thing he knew, he woke up on the uncovered bed to find John Thomas still languishing in his hand, the TV buzzing – and a nice cup of breakfast tea on the bedside table, discreetly put there by his mum as usual.

Another version sets the lad in that ever-popular first-meeting-with-the-girlfriend's-parents scenario. And it's the future in-law who gets an eyeful when she silently brings up the cuppa. Those of a sensitive nature might prefer to think over that embarrassing situation rather than read the next one.

mr Blobby *on the job*

A woman set up her husband for one of those impromptu home invasions Noel Edmonds' shows specialise in while she was 'out with her mates' one Saturday evening. On the show, the cameras burst in and start filming, to the surprise of their unsuspecting prey.

The TV crew secretly case the joint before they begin filming to make sure things run smoothly, and this time it was a good job they did. With the wife who'd contacted them standing nearby, the production crew peered through the living room curtains to check what their victim was up to and make sure he didn't suspect anything.

It was quite soon clear the husband wasn't expecting anything, let alone a TV crew to burst in and film him.

For him it was just another Saturday night without the missus. He was sitting on the couch with his trousers and underpants down, holding a can of beer and playing with himself while watching *Baywatch*.

And – sorry about this – yet another couple of self-gratification stories. Firstly a quickie about a friend of a friend, who as a pubescent teenager used to lie in his bath watching a woman through the bathroom skylight in a flat opposite. Even though she seemed to be looking at him, the mature lady was quite clearly oblivious to his voyeurism and used to undress virtually every time he had a bath. Naturally, he would excitedly stimulate himself accordingly. When he grew up, he became a respectable surveyor for the local council and happened one day to be working on the estate where he'd grown up, now deserted. As a sort of pilgrimage, he paid a visit to the flat of the woman of his childhood dreams. He was quite disturbed when he did, for he found out that from the spot where she would stand and disrobe, his old bathtub was completely exposed to her gaze.

rub-*a*-*dub*

A spotty teenage youth from Kent was enjoying a long languid bath and, having soaped and scoured himself, had begun to get quite aroused.

Needless to say, he decided to relieve himself while still soaking. So he leant on his arm until his hand went dead (that way he could pretend someone else was doing it), and finished the job.

But just as he climaxed, his mum knocked forcefully on the door and told him to hurry up. She wanted to use the same bath to save water (there was a shortage), and she was in a rush. Appalled that his mum would see the conspicuous floating evidence of his vice, the young man spent a frenzied two minutes stalling her while he fished out the flotsam. When he'd done so to his satisfaction, he rushed out and let her in.

Happily, there was not a peep from his mum. But nine months later, the lad had mixed feelings about his mother giving birth to a new brother for him.

the unkindest *cut (again)*

A friend who's a doctor tells the story about a family who were friends as well as patients. One day the wife complained of pains 'down below', and consulted the GP over the matter.

A few days later, the doctor and the wife's other half were out playing tennis one morning. They enjoyed a good hard game, and in the bar afterwards the husband inquired about the problem his wife had had.

'Oh, it was nothing, really,' said the doc. 'She just had a condom lodged in her vagina, nothing to worry about.'

'Oh yes there is,' said the fuming husband. 'You may recall I had the snip three years ago.'

the genital *touch*

There used to be a pub in Newcastle-upon-Tyne just off the notorious Bigg Market cattle-run that had rock'n'roll as its theme, but in a sordid, downmarket way – tacky pictures of Elvis, Eddie Cochran and Tommy Steele, I seem to remember.

But the main attractions in this rowdy drinker were the waitresses, dressed in scanty swimsuits. Every so often the lasses were made to dance, gyrate and cavort on top of the bar to certain songs on a backing tape, with the lusty hordes clapping along with their tongues hanging out.

Apparently, one night, following a particularly exuberant hoofing display, one of the waitresses, who happened to have active genital herpes at the time, rearranged her costume. Then she immediately resumed serving the leering punters, unwittingly passing her affliction on to every cocktail and pint glass she handled.

As a consequence, thirty or so men contracted clusters of genital herpes around their mouths – something, you can imagine, quite difficult to explain away to their partners . . .

> That one's been cruising the bars all over the country. Any regional variations? We'd love to hear them.
>
> The next tale of feminine frailty is a very popular new twist on the 'Surprise!' stories we featured in *Urban Myths*.

her *pedigree chum*

A Surrey businesswoman woke up on her 40th birthday with the usual misgivings and feelings about advancing years. A divorcee, she received just a few cards from her family and went to work feeling very lonely.

At work, no one seemed to have remembered her big day, and no one even asked her out for a celebratory drink at lunchtime or the evening – in fact, they all seemed to leave early.

So she trudged home forlornly, and went through the side gate and round the back into her kitchen as was her habit.

Unknown to her, all her workmates and neighbours had arranged a surprise party for her and were lying in wait in a hushed huddle in the living room.

But when she didn't emerge from the kitchen for twenty minutes, the organiser, her next-door neighbour, decided to check she was all right.

So she sneaked over and eased open the louvre doors to take a peek.

There, lying naked on the floor, was the blue-stocking birthday girl, with dog food smeared all over her body and her pet Labrador enthusiastically licking it off.

whose *baby?*

Some close personal friends of a local wine-bar soak got themselves tied up in a web of complications.

The couple in question had a very active sex life and the

bloke, especially, liked to try out different things to maintain his interest.

He wasn't exactly impotent, but had recently encountered problems rousing himself. After trying all the usual fetishes, one night he suggested to his partner that they try a threesome to spice things up a bit.

His girlfriend wasn't too keen at first, but came round eventually when her man put forward a Jamaican mate, for whom he knew she had a soft spot.

The unusual arrangement seemed to suit them all and went on for a number of weeks until the woman discovered she was pregnant.

Given his own shortcomings, the jealous boyfriend was convinced it was his mate's doing. After a huge bust-up the bloke stormed off. The mate didn't want to know either and the poor woman was left in the lurch with a baby on board.

Being of a decisive turn of mind she determined to find a father for her child, and toured the local nightclubs until she found a suitable candidate.

Luckily he was a lovely bloke and fell for her immediately. And given the way society is, she was happy he was also black.

The bloke was overjoyed when he found his new girl was pregnant, and proposed immediately. After a few months of wedded bliss, the woman had an effortless delivery, and gave birth to a big healthy bouncing baby boy . . . who was also unmistakeably white.

black *pride and joy*

A shy girl who works with a friend's wife in the City was getting married to her childhood sweetheart, back home at their quaint country village church in Kent, the garden of England.

The girls where she worked were forever teasing her about her hen night, but she just reddened and claimed she didn't approve of such things, and would rather spend a quiet night at home crocheting.

Her workmates had other ideas and near the big day practically kidnapped the blushing bride-to-be and took her for a night on the town.

The poor girl was unused to strong liquor and was soon giggly and emotional. They trawled the Covent Garden pubs and wine bars until closing time desperately trying to get the girl chatted up, but to no avail.

Then one of the brasher girls led them to a nightclub she knew just around the corner. They piled in just as the floor show was starting, and screamed their hearts out as an exotic black dancer took the floor and began shedding his already scanty clothing to the strains of 'Simply the Best' by Tina Turner.

As he revealed his musk-oiled and athletic torso, the betrothed could hardly look, but then emboldened by the drink peeped through her fingers at the horny hunk.

The rest of the night was a hazy blur.

The wedding went off without a hitch. The idyllic Norman church made a perfect background for the photographs, and both sets of parents were chuffed to mintballs.

A few weeks later the bride proudly announced she was expecting a baby, and it seemed a marriage made in heaven.

But nine months later the couple split up after evidence of her pre-marital dalliance – the young wife's bundle of joy was born black.

> There are many variations of this black-white theme, most of them showing barely disguised bigotry. Another classic racial stereotype story, but with a moral sting in its tail, is related in the first *Urban Myths*. It's the tale of the black man in the hotel lift shouting 'Hit the deck, lady' and traumatising two prim English tourists. They throw all their money at him thinking he's a mugger, but when they check out of the hotel it transpires that their bill has been paid, their money returned, and there's a note saying that the black man was only telling his dog to sit. Since the book, the LA riots have happened, and inevitably similar stories have arisen centred around the disturbances. So far, the wronged black man has been said to be Eddie Murphy, Lionel Ritchie, Bill Cosby, 'Iron' Mike Tyson and Lovelace Watkins (okay, so we lied about one of them . . .).
>
> But it cuts both ways, naturally: there are plenty of stories of black mothers giving birth to 'throwback' white babies . . .

wart *a secret*

A woman social worker based in Stratford-upon-Avon used to look after a lovely old lady in her late seventies who never wanted to put anyone out, and so was allowing herself gradually to deteriorate physically.

But the social worker was particularly concerned about one major affliction her charge suffered from – genital warts.

Over the weeks and months, the woman had persistently waved away any suggestion that she should have her affliction checked over by a quack, though the social worker was increasingly anxious something should be done. Eventually, she settled on asking the elegant woman why not. After stalling again and again, the proud old lady was moved close to tears.

'I can't! I'm too embarrassed!' she sobbed.

'But why? It's nothing to be ashamed of,' reassured the carer.

'Oh but it *is* . . . because they'll know what I've been doing,' said the woman, holding out her unsightly, blemished fingers.

A friend who works in the animation industry claims that he is personally responsible for the introduction of a now virulent urban myth. The actual event happened to him a number of years ago, while he was a student in Liverpool, and he related the story to a select few at the time. But recently his brother, who still lives by the Mersey, heard an apocryphal tale bearing a striking resemblance to his brother's experience – only the name had been lost in the countless retellings. When pressed, the woman who was telling the story as though she knew the protagonist intimately admitted that it apparently happened to a friend of a friend.

the party *pooper*

A mate went to art college, leaving home for the first time, and early in the first term he went out to a humdinger of a house party in a dodgy bit of Liverpool.

He'd taken his carrier bag of cheap cooking lager, and soon got into the swing of the drunken revelry. Psychedelic music thumped out, students writhed by the light of joss sticks and – even better – there were *girls* there.

Midway into the evening, the room started to spin. It could have been the lager, or the iffy, fish-scented footy-burger he'd had on the way up, but the freshman's bottom was telling him he was in dire need of the toilet.

The queue for the lav in the house stretched all the way upstairs, but there was no way he could wait (or risk the noise he'd make with people standing outside). Then he remembered there was a small loo downstairs in the hall and made a mad dash.

Happily, it was quiet below the party, though the toilet was fusty and dark. After a noisy delivery, the lad reached for the paper, but – nightmare of all nightmares – there was no bum-fodder.

Terrified of humiliation, he sat there quaking, stinking and thinking hard. Then a drunken thought occurred to him. He took off his paisley Y-fronts and used those as a

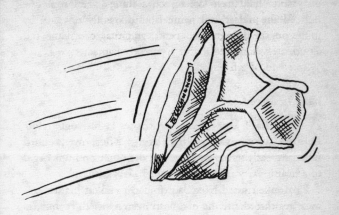

sanitary wipe, flinging them into the porcelain bowl and flushing the handle triumphantly.

But to his horror when the toilet water cleared the soiled shreddies were still there, steaming in the pan. A couple more cistern-busting flushes produced the same result, so he fished out the Y's and tried another method of disposal.

Opening the door a crack and checking there was no one around, he ran through the front door and hurled the sopping, stained knickers out into the street. Minutes later he was back upstairs in the party humming, convinced he'd got away with it.

Later as he and his new mates were leaving, they came across a gaggle of party people on the pavement and strolled over.

The students were gathered around a heavily-soiled pair of sodden paisley underpants and discussing what sort of dirty sod could have done such a thing. Then someone noticed the old school name label diligently sewn in by mum on the hem of the pants, and read the name out aloud . . .

balls *bounced*

A friend has a story about two mates at his rugby club. One day, the two were having a post-match shower as usual when one of them bent over, and the other one was heard to exclaim, 'Cor, the size of your ball-bag, mate.'

The embarrassed bloke was forced to admit his secret – by a freak of nature, he had been overendowed, by one, in the testicular department.

When he'd recovered his composure, the other fellow suddenly had an idea. At the pub they were going to, there was a barman who would bet on absolutely anything, no matter how impossible – he was a bookies' dream, a real mug punter. The bloke hit upon a scheme to earn them free drinks all night.

They arrived at the boozer and the insatiable Billy Bunter barman was there for the taking. They played it cool for a minute, then the rugger player leaned over the bar and whispered into the barman's ear: 'Betcha, between you and my mate, you've got five bollocks.'

The barman gave him an old-fashioned look. He repeated the bet. The barman began to smile, and the bloke knew he'd got him.

They settled on a wager, and the barman disappeared into the toilet, followed by the three-ball rugby player.

But to his surprise the barman swiftly undid his kecks

and dropped them, saying defiantly, 'There's my one, where are your four?'

potato *stew*

A young Irish woman, known to a friend of a workmate, was one of those particularly naive types that only the county of Kerry appears to produce. She was from a small village, but had the womanly urges of a lusty city-dweller.

One day, at the tender age of sixteen, she asked her friend for some advice.

She said that she was knocking around with a lovely boy who really loved her, and was desperate to make love with her. But despite her real desire to satiate his passion, she was a good Catholic and wouldn't use contraception, so was terrified she would get pregnant.

Her friend passed on some advice a knowing old crone in the village had once secretly given: slip a spud inside you to block the appropriate tubes, and you'll never get pregnant. And as a potato is one of God's vegetables, it couldn't possibly count as contraception.

The young Kerrywoman followed this advice and enjoyed a fulfilling sex life with her lover for some months, with never a hint of conception, even though she was still using the same spud.

However, she had begun to feel pains in her stomach and decided to see a doctor. Before the visit she set about removing her barrier method. After quite a few tugs, the potato finally popped out, and she was happy the doctor, a friend of her mother's, wouldn't be any the wiser.

However, after a brief external examination, the medic

suggested an internal might be in order to find the source of the pains. A few moments into it he fell back shocked and bewildered.

The young woman screamed at him to tell her what he saw.

'I haven't seen anything like it in years,' he stammered. 'You've got the branches of a potato plant growing out of your ovaries.'

> Beware the root that is all evil – some of you will recall from our first book the story of the tomato plant growing in the nasal cavity, but we reckon the spud contraceptive eggseeds that by far. (Sorry.)

massage *virgin*

A friend of a bloke I know works in an insurance office, where he sits opposite a portly middle-aged bloke with sweat permanently peppering his top lip.

This shiny-arse was a bit of a hypochondriac and was never slow to complain about his ailments. His regular gripe was a painful ache between his shoulder blades, brought on he reckoned by his high stress duties – paper shuffling.

A workmate sick to the back teeth of the malingerer's whining suggested he try a massage to relieve the tension and recommended a place nearby. The bloke was hesitant at first but said he'd give it a try. That lunchtime he popped out early in search of relief.

The massage parlour was just off the high street: it looked clean and bright, and the professional neon sign was most encouraging, so he scuttled inside. He was soon flat on his belly with only a towel to preserve his modesty.

The lithely-built oriental masseuse got stuck in straight away, kneading and pummelling in all the right places. To the bloke's astonishment, the pain disappeared almost immediately and he began to relax and thoroughly enjoy the massage. So relaxed was he in fact, that the firm hands working on his body started to have a stimulating effect, and he was soon feeling more than a little aroused.

When the comely masseuse asked him to flip over she couldn't help noticing his conspicuous excitement. So she whispered furtively in his ear, 'Would you like a wank?'

The bloke thought for a second, then nodded furiously.

The masseuse winked and left the room, and the bloke lay back, his head filled with mucky thoughts awaiting her return in who knows what exotic costume.

But a few minutes later, the masseuse popped her head round the door and said, 'Have you finished yet?'

He obviously got the wrong end of the stick.

mythellaneous

Sex

* It's got a bone in it
* Oriental ones go sideways
* Ra-Ra-Rasputin, Russia's greatest love machine, was actually impotent. A doctor who examined him in 1915 found his 'parts' shrivelled
* Some sheep-shaggers turn the animal round in their wellies so as not to miss out on the kissing
* Shag a sheep on a cliff: it backs up
* In the First World War, two-thirds of the men fighting had some form of venereal disease
* Legendary porn actor King Dong fainted through lack of blood when his pendulous member became erect
* The large penis gene is dominant, and as a people we are getting bigger
* Most blokes could tell you where the 'G-spot' is
* Gerbils are the most popular pets in the whole of California
* The Kama Sutra was first translated by nuns
* Whenever there's a power cut, nine months later there's a population explosion; the biggest baby boom ever occurred nine months after England won the World Cup in 1966

that's *showbiz*

Stars and tripe

Wonderful world, beautiful people . . . Fame is a double-edged sword, as this ripping set of celebrity scares shows. The glitterati may have the one-liners, the fame, the fortune and the facelifts, but we've got the rumours.

'e always *calls me that*

Leo Abse, the celebrated writer and biographer, pronounces his name 'Ab*see*', as anyone who's eaten canapés with him is of course aware. But he was once invited to give a talk to a very small literary club in Middlesbrough about one of his biographies, and although he had his doubts, he decided to accept.

When he saw how small-time it was his doubts resumed. The chairman was affable enough, a bluff, no-nonsense Yorkshireman, but he wondered whether it had been worth the trip.

Anyway, the chairman set things in motion by giving Abse the big build-up. The only problem was that in his introduction, he persistently referred to the writer as Mr Leo 'Abs'. Abse leaned over and said with as much of a smile as he could manage, 'Actually, it's Ab*see*.'

'Lovely,' pronounced his host, 'and you can call me "Jonesy".'

what *a shower*

A British heavy metal band, one stage more preposterous than Spinal Tap, were touring eastern Europe recently.

As part of the climax to their scintillating live act – all gothic imagery, juicing hogs and hi-energy guitar solos, the lead singer, who loved his fans and really respected them, would spray the front rows of the stadium with water from a hose to cool them down.

But the British roadies were contemptuous of the newly-liberated states' overenthusiastic fans, who they believed didn't truly understand what metal was all about.

So they spent a week stockpiling their urine (and they produce a lot, these beer-bandits) in a spare water tank. When the tank was full, they connected it to the lead singer's hose in place of the usual source.

At the next football stadium they played, as the show built up to its peak and the sweating audience were going wild, the unwitting frontman showered his adoring fans with the roadies' pungent, stale urine.

> Another version of this tale suggests, implausibly, that when Tommy Steele starred in the London West End stage version of 'Singing In The Rain', he had made such an impression on the stage crew that when the hugely successful play was set finally to close, each of them allegedly made a deposit every night into a central fund to give him a present on the curtain-closing night. The only problem was that, reportedly, the deposit was urine, and the fund was the reservoir normally used for the rainwater required during the story's most famous umbrella-twirling scene.
>
> Sadly, as legend has it, on the final night when the cheerful Cockney star was singing in the rain, it really *was* pissing it down.

coping *with adversity*

In the wild and wicked world of rock'n'roll, the excesses of the red-blooded members of popular bands are well documented, notably in the 'rider', that part of the concert contract containing the 'extras' demanded by the band.

They might ask for six litres of whisky in their dressing room, four courses of 'Ital' (or even Italian) food, substantial amounts of something for the nose (a typical line), or 'something for the weekend', thinking they'll strike lucky with a groupie. Other rockers are known for their more sedate, eccentric riders, and one apocryphal story stands out.

Julian Cope, the earthy, intellectual singer from indie group The Teardrop Explodes, supposedly had it written into every live performance contract that the venue must supply 'a dark, quiet room backstage with a copy of the Bible in it'.

For the big venues, the only problem was how to get hold of a copy of the good book. For a small-time polytechnic, though, the facilities were far too limited.

When faced with an angry Cope a few hours before curtain-up one night when the singer's solo career was at its peak, the ents officer at a London polytechnic had the choice of finding some non-existent backstage room or waving bye-bye to the temperamental singer and facing the wrath of hundreds of livid students who'd come to see him.

Luckily, the ents bloke was resourceful. He told Cope he'd found a room, and asked him to follow. He led him as far as a tiny toilet and pointed to a Bible he'd put on top of the toilet roll.

'But it's not dark,' muttered Cope.

So the student reached up and unscrewed the light bulb.

'Excellent,' smiled Cope, giving him a satisfied thumbs-up.

tip *off*

Tommy Cooper, one of the funniest men Britain has ever produced, was apparently, like many clowns, sad at heart.

Not only that, but he was allegedly tight-fisted, too.

Once, when he hailed a cab to take him from outside his home to the television studios, it turned out the cabbie – salt o' the earth – was a big fan, and was knocked out to have his hero 'in the back'.

The cabbie treated his 'fare' to a rendition of all his own best jokes and sketches. The TV funnyman seemed a proper gent, even joining in on a few lines, despite being at the height of his success.

As they pulled up outside the studios (some time later than expected – cabbies drive slower when they're enjoying themselves), the lugubrious comic got out and paid the fare.

Then he pulled a clenched fist from his trouser pocket and indicated that he was offering a substantial tip. The cabbie was made up.

'Here's a drink for you and your mates,' said Cooper, stuffing his closed hand into the cab driver's top pocket.

Later on, the cabbie was having his lunch when he remembered the comedian's gratuity. He reached into his pocket to see how much it was – he'd been too embarrassed to look at the time.

But he had to laugh when his idol's tip turned out to be . . . two teabags.

> That 'drink for you and your mates' story has also been heard about another financially astute comic, Ken Dodd.

hitched *up*

Allegedly the late great Alfred Hitchcock was a right practical joker, and no mistake, but a vicious streak often put a nasty sting in the tail of his japes.

One one occasion during the filming of *Psycho* he is said to have been geed up by one of the technicians that the set wasn't scary enough. Hitchcock threw down a gauntlet to the cheeky chap, betting him he'd be too frightened to spend a night tied to a chair on the set with all the lights out. The bloke took up the challenge, and when he was safely fastened by rope to the chair, Hitchcock generously offered him a nightcap to make him sleep better.

But the drink contained a wicked double dose of strong laxative.

In the morning, when the first workers arrived on set, they found the poor technician a jibbering, sobbing wreck, still strapped in the chair, wishing he'd worn his bicycle clips.

best *for Last*

In the late seventies, a friend of a friend's father took over as the entertainments officer of a small but popular working men's club in Cumbria.

His job was dead easy as there were always plenty of people at the events he booked – mostly there for bellyfuls of cheap beer – and the place only held a couple of hundred.

Towards the end of the financial year, the club's accountant reported that they'd made a big profit, nearly £15,000.

He also suggested that unless they spent the surplus, it would all go to the taxman. So the committee asked the ents officer to book the biggest act he could for a special night to use up the surplus. The entertainments officer found himself dealing with artists and agents in a much bigger league than his usual batch of nightclub singers and stand-ups when he rang around with his requirements, but he seemed to carry it off, and pretty soon the offers started trickling in.

Someone phoned offering Shirley Bassey for £5,000. 'Not enough,' replied the ents man, lording it up, 'We're talking *big* bucks.'

Another agent rang saying that Lovelace Watkins was available in a package with Peter Gordeno and his dancers for seven and a half grand. 'Small beer!' snapped the WMC man smugly. 'Get me something top-drawer!'

The next day, he was offered some of the top names in light entertainment in one billing: Norman Collier, Tony Monopoly and Freddie 'Parrot Face' Davies. 'How much?' snapped the ents man.

'Nine big ones,' replied the agent.

'Not enough, I need to pay more,' said the bloke.

'Well, I've got James Last, full show, going out for £13,000,' suggested the agent.

'Never heard of him, but the price is right. Done.'

Come the big night, the events officer was waiting outside his little club when James Last's Rolls-Royce rolled up ahead of his cortege – an articulated lorry and several vans.

The bloke ran over to greet him, shook his hand and said 'Right, Mr Last, are you self-contained or d'you need the house trio?'

stand-up *and be counted*

Someone I met on holiday in Corfu knew a bloke at work who was trying to make it as a stand-up comedian.

The main problem he had was ... timing, and that's quite crucial when you're a comic. But his material was bad too, and he had no stage presence either. His friends at work ruthlessly ribbed him, saying things like 'How did the operation go?'

The bloke would ask what operation they were on about.

'The charisma bypass operation, of course,' they'd all shout, collapsing with laughter.

But the would-be Tarby managed to get a few club dates over the years, and sometimes his mates would turn up, shouting 'Give up your day job!'

His big break came when he landed a weekly residency at a big Working Men's Club in Halifax. The place was known for its tough audience and intolerance of poor material, but the bloke took his chances and worked the hardest he'd ever done in preparing his routine – he even bought some Bernard Manning videos to try out some of the jokes from that.

Come the big first night, the bloke was waiting, clammy-palmed, in the wings for the big build-up from the compere.

'As some of you will know,' began the brash clubman, 'I've just today taken over from Nobby, who was sacked for doing such a bad job as the club's entertainments officer.'

Then he paused for maximum impact, before continuing gravely, 'So hopefully this next bloke will be the last crap act we have on here ...'

oh *oh dear*

During the 1992 election, Scottish film actor Sean Connery made clear his support for the Nationalists in his homeland and wrote letters from his luxurious southern Spanish home in their support.

Understandably, many Scots newspapers were keen to clinch an interview with the former James Bond star, but he wanted to let his political pronouncements do the talking for him.

However, after much harassment, he consented to doing just one exclusive interview for the sister newspaper of the *Mirror*, the *Scottish Daily Record*. But he made it known that he wanted to approve the quotes used before the interview was printed, and the *Record* agreed to his demand. The *Sun*, the *Mirror*'s deadly rival north and south of the border, was absolutely livid at this slight, and set about spoiling tactics.

As it happened, one member of the *Sun*'s London editorial staff in Fortress Wapping did a passable 'Mush Monneypanny' Fountain Bridge brogue like Edinburgh-born Connery, and it was decided that he should have a stab at winding the *Record*'s staff up. The *Sun* impersonator rang the *Record*'s offices at one in the morning, told the switchboard who he was and was put through to a lowly sub-editor.

'Mr Connery' explained he was ringing from Spain and was very annoyed he hadn't been contacted about the feature and the quotes which were to be used. The sub reasoned that the feature wasn't going to run for a couple of days, so it was a little early for that, but the intimidating impersonator brushed such trifles aside and said that unless

211

a transcript of the whole interview was read to him over the phone for approval, he would not give his consent and the feature would never run.

With the naivety of one new to the wiles of the hot metal profession, the sub searched through computer files until he found the full Sean Connery interview transcript and innocently read it verbatim, and very slowly, down the phone to his paper's arch rival.

The *Sun* duly published their exclusive feature on Sean Connery, scooping the newspaper that had done the interview. Needless to say, the *Record*'s young sub was sacked.

> Sub-editors, those meddlers with journalists' precious scribblings, have been the butt of many a Fleet Street joke throughout the years, and tend to create their own, well, 'sub culture' at newspapers. Some time back the *Guardian* subs are said to have run a competition between themselves to see who could repeat a chosen phase the most times over a week, with a substantial bounty in drinks to the winner. One week, the selected phrase they had to 'implant' was 'and they all wore skirts'.
>
> Several managed to sneak it in here and there – describing striking miners on picket, that sort of thing – but one bloke in his last-ever shift, who'd never won the challenge, ran the phrase 100 times down a column – but it didn't count because it was spotted and changed after the first edition.

shanks' *phoney*

Bill Shankly, the man who said football wasn't a matter of
life and death – 'It's more important than that' – had an
accent barely penetrable to anyone south of Glasgow. Even
after years working down south, it could lead to misunder-
standings, even official ones.

At the start of the Second World War, all young men of
eligible age had to register their occupation so the call-up
could exclude workers in 'nationally important' occupations.

Shanks was playing football in England, and when a
toffee-nosed Sassenach jobsworth came to interview him
and asked him his line of work, he replied in his lightest
brogue that he was a footballer.

Some time later, Shankly received official notification
that he was ineligible for call-up because 'Fruit-Boiler' was
a job vital to the country's wartime needs.

> The same funny-Scottish-accent-leading-to-
> fruitboiler-profession was connected with Celtic
> ace Dixie Dean. For some reason, there are a
> number of myths surrounding once-glorious
> Chelsea FC (not least that they used to be
> glorious).

bridge *of sighs*

In 1966, when Chelsea were due to play an important
European cup match, the first leg was due to take place at
Stamford Bridge. But Blues manager Tommy Docherty

decided he wanted to play away first, so that his lads knew what they had to do in the home leg.

Mysteriously, on the eve of the Bridge rendezvous, the local fire brigade flooded the Chelsea pitch – unbeknown to the match referee, who ruled it unplayable, and abandoned the tie until after the away leg.

Had he taken the time to ring the London weather centre, he would have suspected foul play – no rainfall had been registered on the night in question.

In the European Cup Winners Cup Final in Athens, 1971, Chelsea drew with Real Madrid, and had to stay at their hotel until the replay.

On the eve of the return match, young Alan Hudson found ace striker Peter Osgood knocking back the beers in the bar like nobody's business.

'Ossie,' said Hudson, 'what are you doing – it's the final tomorrow!'

Straight-faced, Osgood replied, 'It's not the final, Alan, it's only the replay.'

> The computer hasn't yet been built that can store all the weird and wonderful stories surrounding the legendary businessman Robert Maxwell and his antics. One, however, has truly taken on proportions worthy of the man himself – big in every way.

going *overboard*

One day at the Mirror Group offices in Holborn, London, Robert Maxwell, who lived in the luxurious penthouse flat at the top, was coming down in the lift. At the next floor he was joined by a scruffy young lad in a suit, who happened to be smoking.

Maxwell was furious that one of his employees should be flouting the company's no-smoking policy – it was a pet hate of his – and he made his feelings known, gruffly telling the office boy to extinguish the weed. The lad sneered and paid no attention, taking another deep draw on his fag and blowing the smoke towards the intimidating entrepreneur.

Maxwell was absolutely livid at this menial's disobedience, and again angrily insisted that he put out the cigarette immediately. The cheeky young man spat 'No!' back at him and carried on puffing.

At this, Maxwell furiously demanded to know how much the young man earned a week. 'Two hundred quid. Why?' scowled the young scamp, as the lift doors opened to the lobby.

'Because,' boomed the magnate, fishing £400 from his pocket and handing it to the bewildered lad, 'I'm giving you two weeks' notice. You're fired! Get out of this building now!'

'Don't worry, mate!' chuckled the rascal, fleeing through the doors with his wad, 'I work for Telecom, anyway!'

last *for Best*

When my uncle re-upholstered George Best's discotheque he heard a curious tale.

George, or Georgie as he was then known, had hit the heights with Manchester United in the late sixties but by the mid-seventies was sadly on the slippery slope down from his former greatness.

A cub reporter keen to cash in on George's fall from grace somehow managed to fix up an interview with the football genius at a swanky London hotel.

The day of the scoop interview arrived, and the reporter turned up on the dot, knocking gently on the hotel room door. It was opened by the great man himself, wearing only a bath towel, beard unkempt and looking well below par.

The reporter entered the room littered with empty champagne bottles. The bed was rumpled, and girlish laughter echoed from the bathroom.

George had been spotted the night before out on the town with yet another newly-crowned Miss World, and judging from the sash and flowers strewn on the deck, one thing had clearly led to another and George hadn't had a wink all night.

The reporter surveyed the scene before him. Then flipping open his note book, he licked his pencil and asked the bemused Best, 'Well, George, where did it all go wrong?'

quite *Frankly*

A friend of a friend knows a bloke who was once in a Las Vegas nightclub with a young woman to see the marvellous Frank Sinatra in concert. He'd contrived to have a table close to the stairs where 'old blue eyes' walked up to the stage.

Just before Frank was due to go on, the bloke managed to blag his way backstage and talk to the great singer. He explained that his name was Bill, and he'd met Sinatra in the very same club ten years ago when they'd had a drink after the show.

Since that time, the bloke said, he'd married a young lady, but right now they were going through a very rough patch, and he'd taken the liberty of saying he knew Mr Sinatra really well.

'Frank,' said Bill, 'I'm real sorry to put upon you like this, but if you could just say "Hi" or something as you walk to the stage, it would really impress her, and raise her opinion of me, maybe even save our marriage.'

Being an affable sort of guy, Frankie agreed to do so, and as he walked to the stage with the spotlight on him, he leaned over the table where Bill was canoodling with his lady companion and said, 'Hi Bill, long time no see, how are things?'

Bill turned around scowling and snarled loudly, 'Piss off Frank, can't you see I'm busy?'

mythellaneous

Filthy lucre

✶ The Bank of England has to buy one of every new photocopier, fax or computer printer to test how well they can forge notes

✶ You can fully recharge phone cards by putting them in the freezer overnight

✶ Hamburgers are stolen and used as hard currency in Russia

✶ It's offensive to tip in Japan, especially judges

✶ If you write a cheque in green ink and then fold it, it takes ten days to clear

✶ The ink for US dollar bills comes from crushed butterfly wings

✶ There have been hushed-up cases of a person using a hole-in-the-wall cash machine and it has accidentally spewed out hundreds of pounds

✶ In California, the dollar bills last half the time they do in other parts of the USA – they get worn out because they're so often used for snorting 'nose candy'

✶ An ancient law, still valid but little used, states that if you accost someone in the street and can correctly guess how much money they have in their pocket, you can keep it

occupational *hazards*

Nine-to-five nonsense

Work, rest and pray is the message of this set of industrial revelations. From paper shuffling and nursing the chronic to naval manoeuvres – whatever you do for a living, the fickle finger of fate is always at work. Earning a crust has never been so risky. Never mind taking care of business, just take care of number one . . .

super *fly guy*

In the seventies, our uncle, a mere stripling in the field of employment, landed a job as an assistant in an anglers' shop in Norwich. He was keen and thorough, and the boss loved him for it. So it wasn't long before the lad found himself holding the fort for his employer while the boss went off drinking, philandering or, very occasionally, fishing.

Needless to say, it wasn't long before the boss started to take the . . . well, take advantage, and explained that he'd be off Saturday and Monday due to a long weekend's engagement with a young lady he was instructing in the noble art of fly fishing. So saying, he entrusted his young assistant with the responsibility of locking up the shop at the weekend.

Saturday arrived quickly, and after a brisk day's trade, the lad flipped the sign round to 'closed', cashed up, swept up and turned off all the switches.

Come Monday morning, the keen youth was up with the lark and back at work to open up for trading. He opened the shutters, checked the till and unlocked the door.

The first customer wanted some maggots, so he popped round the back to get them from the cold store.

But when he opened the heavy door, he was immediately made aware of the dangers of turning off the fridge by mistake – a huge cloud of bluebottles flew straight at him, swarming directly into his gaping mouth and choking him.

a miner *tiff*

A mate's dad used to be a pitman in one of the Welsh collieries along with his mates from the same village.

One evening they'd finished a hard day's back-breaking toil, mining a narrow seam deep, deep down in the bowels of the earth. And after crawling half a mile or so back on their bellies, they hitched a lift back to the surface standing on the top of the lift cage, as miners do when there are a lot of others also wanting to fill their lungs with fresh air.

But as the creaking elevator neared daylight, the motor stuttered and the cage, loaded with miners, lurched horribly and violently sideways.

One of the pitmen on top was caught off balance by the

movement. He lost his footing and fell off the lift, down towards a mile and a half of pitch-black mine shaft and certain death.

But a quick-witted faceworker in the cage below swiftly lunged over the side, risking his own life to grab down and catch the tumbling miner by the hair – the only part he was able to reach in time. He held on painfully until the others were able to scramble to both workers' aid.

Once safely on the surface, the two men – saved and saviour – locked in a hearty and tearful embrace, and everyone cheered.

Understandably, the event cemented their friendship. They were always talking about each other, visiting and going out drinking. In fact they became inseparable.

But exactly one month after the near-fatal accident, the miner who'd fallen noticed that where his mate had grabbed his hair to save him, the locks were now tumbling out.

Within a day, as if it was in delayed shock, his entire lustrous head of hair was lost. He became as bald as a coot and the hair never grew back.

From that day forward he never again spoke to the man who'd saved his life.

playing *away*

A middle-aged travelling salesman from Salford found himself spending the night in Finsbury Park, north London.

Being frugal with his brass, he sought out a suitably downmarket hotel opposite the park to kip down, though understandably charged his company for a night in a more salubrious venue.

Despite the ropey nature of the hotel, the salesman still wanted the best for his money and tried it on by asking for something 'a bit special, please' when he checked in. The flouncy receptionist winked and said, 'Would you like an extra pillow, sir?'

'Let me see how I get on with what I've got first,' replied the bloke.

Then he went upstairs, pushing his way along the corridor occupied by a number of women chatting with what appeared, by the age differences, to be their fathers. He found his room to be a dim, austere single with a clapped-out telly.

Still, he was knackered and it was late, so he flopped down in front of the blinking goggle box.

An hour later, he was ready for bed. Ignoring the dubious round hole carved in the middle of the mattress halfway up, he put his head down. But the pillow was like a sack of marbles, and extremely uncomfortable. He tossed and turned, then eventually rang reception.

'I'll have an extra pillow now, please,' he told the receptionist.

Five minutes later, there was a knock at the door. When he opened it, a voluptuous young lady walked in, smiled and began slowly undressing.

Flustered, the stammering bloke asked her what she thought she was doing.

'You rang for me, didn't you?' she replied coyly.

Apparently, as she explained it, the code in many London hotels for engaging female company for the night is to ask for 'an extra pillow'.

'Damn,' said the salesman, 'shame I didn't ask for two pillows like I normally have.'

Hotels, of course, are better known for what's stolen from them rather than what's provided. It's very common for TVs to go walkies, and mini-bars are there for the taking. (And we thought it was just cutlery and towels.)

Odder, though, were the findings in a survey last year of what's *left* in British hotels. Apparently, it disclosed that the most commonly abandoned item is, overwhelmingly, the 'girlie magazine'. Next came spectacles and odd socks, and one hotel even reported an unclaimed false leg. Presumably a miraculous recovery had taken place.

the big *welcome*

A small hotel near Keswick was finding it hard to compete with the more upmarket and historic old country guest houses nearby, and the crotchety owner came to the conclusion that he would have to appeal to the snob in people if he was going to make a go of it.

The simplest and cheapest thing he could do straight away to give some distinction to the place was to swap his denuded old welcome mat for a brand new top-quality doormat with a large family crest on it. It would be the first impression people got as they walked through the door – and first impressions are so important.

But it didn't go as smoothly as the hotel manager hoped. He rang a company that specialised in prestige doormats, and described what he wanted.

The salesman at the other end of the line asked him how

big he wanted it. 'The usual size,' said the hotel owner, a little tetchily.

'Sir, you don't seem to understand. We make doormats for some of the biggest hotels and company offices in the country, as well as small domestic ones. Perhaps you could quickly measure up and tell us what you want.'

The bad-tempered owner refused to get down on his knees for such a menial and, in his view, pointless task. 'Why are you being so stupid about this?' he roared, exasperated. 'Just make it bloody door-sized!'

Another headache was the extortionate price the makers were asking, but the hotel boss reasoned, after much deliberation, that you've got to speculate to accumulate, and agreed to it.

Three weeks later the doormat arrived, beautifully woven with the manager's family crest and immaculately finished.

There was just one problem; it was huge. In fact, it was as big as the door itself and wouldn't fit in the hotel lobby.

When the furious hotel owner rang to complain, the manufacturers politely pointed out that they were just following instructions: the doormat was, after all, the size of the door.

the navy *lark*

Some years back, a Royal Navy frigate arrived at the naval base in Malta after a long tour of duty, and the crew were grateful when the captain announced that because of the demanding nature of recent weeks, they would be allowed an extra day's shore leave.

Unhappily, quite a few of the jolly tars drank the skipper's health a little too often, and were three sheets to the wind by the time they had to rush back to beat the curfew.

The best taxis in Malta have always been the 'gharries', garishly painted horse-drawn carts often festooned with lights and raucous bells, but they were not always the most reliable – particularly if the horse was a month off being dog-meat, as was often sadly the case.

Often the tardy tars, anxious to avoid a night in the brig, would encourage a gharrie driver to speed up his animal by extending a carrot in front of its nose, or plying it with a local beer made from sea water – you can imagine what effect that had on the poor horse.

Anyhow, this particular night was one of those occasions when a lot of seamen needed to be carried back to ship, and pronto. So the gharries were being asked to pull all the stops out, the drivers were trying every shortcut, and the horses were being whipped and driven into the ground to reach the ship on time.

Nevertheless, the captain was furious to hear that a large number of his crew failed to return by curfew that night. He called all the guilty sailors into his cabin one by one to hear what they had to say in their defence.

'Well,' said the first one nervously, 'the gharrie was coming up to the harbour at an incredible pace because I didn't want to be late, when the horse suddenly pulled up short, keeled over and died.'

'A likely story,' said the skipper, but let him off with a warning.

The next tar told virtually the same story. And the next one, and the next one. In fact, the next five sailors all claimed the horse pulling their gharrie had pegged out under the strain of making it back to the ship.

So when the last late arrival was ushered in, the cynical captain said disdainfully, 'And I suppose your gharrie's horse bit the bullet just as you were arriving at the ship too, did it?'

'No suh!' shouted the stiff but dishevelled sailor.

'Then explain yourself!'

'Well sir, the gharrie was going fine until we got to the harbour . . . and then we couldn't get near the ship for all these dead horses.'

> The following grisly tale puts a whole new twist
> on the idea of Armed Forces cuts . . .

para-*noia*

There is apparently a group of hardcore neo-Nazi para-troopers in the British Army who are so loopy they collect body parts of people they've killed as mementos and keep them in pockets on their utility belts – a new twist on the Native American close crew-cut collections, introduced by Spanish settlers, perhaps.

Among the most prized parts of their vanquished foes are ears (especially), little fingers and of course privates' privates. According to our sources, one para hero in the Falklands was denied a posthumous medal for bravery after a superior officer found a bag of Argentinian human souvenirs in his personal effects.

> Perhaps they're all corporals . . .

capital *hideout*

During his time at art college a mate wanted to go up to the top of the Euston Tower to photograph a panoramic view of London.

Selecting a fiver from his wallet to bribe the doorman, he was about to set off, but was alerted by a friend's acquaintances that he wouldn't be allowed up – it's a little-known fact that the SAS own the top two floors and don't let anyone up there.

Apparently MI5 and the SAS also own parts of Centre Point, the revolving restaurant up the Telecom Tower, and other vantage points around the capital, all perfect for surveillance and abseiling.

> And they say you can't get good office space in London these days. It's an even less well-known fact that MI5 receives copies of every single fax sent from Britain to a foreign country – faxes are easier to bug than telephones. So next time you consider sending a copy of your rear end to a close friend, think on.

the bottle *of Britain*

A friend of a friend who's a pilot in the RAF discovered an interesting secret that's been hushed up for over forty years.

During the dark days of the Second World War, when Hitler's Third Reich cast its fascist shadow across mainland Europe, Britain stood fast against the jackboot of Nazi oppression until eventually the tide of the war started to turn.

Bomber Command's strategy was to pound the Hun into submission and thousands of tons of high explosive were rained down on to the industrial heartland of the Nazi war machine. Day and night, week in week out, the Lancasters and Wellingtons flew sortie after sortie unloading their lethal cargo. Apparently there were so many bombing raids into Germany that the factories couldn't keep up and they ran out of bombs. It would have been a national disaster had the news got out, but luckily the backroom boffins came up with a cunning scheme to maintain the pressure on the Boche until the factories caught up. The RAF switched to dropping empty beer bottles because they whistled just like real bombs on the way down.

Also at this time the government removed the iron railings from working-class areas all over Britain to help with the war effort. Most people thought that due to raw material shortages the cast iron was to be melted down and used to build tanks, ships and planes etc., so they were happy to give up their railings for Britain.

But apparently the whole exercise was dreamt up by the War Office to boost public morale. The railings weren't even melted down, they were collected up, then dumped in the North Sea at night.

Furthermore the ultimate weapon developed and used during the conflict by the Americans, The Bomb, has been responsible for real shortages of its own. Apparently all X-ray machines have to be made from metal reclaimed from pre-Second World War sunken ships because after the first nuclear explosion and all the subsequent atomic testing in

the sixties all terrestrial metals in the world are contaminated by radioactivity.

gull-*able*

Before the HMS *Ark Royal* was recycled into cat-food tins, a schoolmate qualified as an engineer and served on her.

On one especially long and tiresome tour of the South China Seas the ratings discovered a novel, if gruesome pastime.

Apparently, one morning after a particularly riotous drinking session, one of the gunners staggered out on to the deck, struggling to find his sea legs in the heavy seas and dropped some Alka-Seltzer into a glass of water.

The sailor was being pestered by the wheeling gulls as

usual, begging and cawing for food. Without thinking, he hurled a spare tablet at one cackling seabird.

Like lightning, the gull whirled, caught the tablet in its beak and swallowed.

Then it flew a few feet and exploded with a fizzing bang, and Alka-Seltzer became the most popular purchase on every shore leave en route.

right *royal burial*

A naval acquaintance from Plymouth once served on the *Ark Royal*, pride of the British Navy, and had to wipe a salty tear from his eye when the old tub slipped anchor for the last time, after years of valiant service, and steamed out of retirement for the Falklands disaster.

The Treasury axe inevitably fell, and to the tune of Rod Stewart's 'Sailing', the well-loved giant aircraft carrier was scrapped. But not without leaving a mystery in her wake. Apparently she was melted down with the body of a man killed in one of her campaigns still irretrievably lost in her hold.

the missing *link*

A mate and I were playing pool in a pub in Tavistock, Devon. The place was scattered with a few crusty local characters, including one lad who we took for an under-age drinker. He turned out to be a squaddy and was mouthing off about his tank regiment's recent manoeuvres.

'There uz were, out down Salisbury Plain, in the Chieftain loike, when uz come across this inter-village.'

'You what? What's that when 'e's at 'ome?' inquired one of the yokels.

'You know, an inter-bred village. Apparently they were cut off from the outside world when the army acqoired the larnd, so they has to marry each other – brother to sister and that,' explained the private.

'Sounds 'orrible,' gasped one local.

'I dunno . . .' mused another.

'Anyway,' the boy soldier continued, 'nobody knows it's there, so we use it as target practice, taking pot shots at the people and blasting the buildings, loike.'

> Apparently there's another unfortunate inbred village just the same in Norway.

highly *unrealistic*

This is how Soviet 'social realism' in art was born.

Just after the Bolshevik revolution, a powerful sultan in one of the old Russian republics asked a local artist to paint his portrait for posterity. When the excited painter went to visit the sultan, he discovered that he might have a few problems making the picture flattering – the war-scarred VIP subject had one eye, one leg and a hunched back.

The artist decided to gloss over the sultan's shortcomings and satisfy his vanity, so he painted him in a glamorous and stirring scene looking the perfect specimen of manhood, surrounded by beautiful women.

When the sultan saw the fictitious representation, he was furious. How dare the painter make fun of him like that, pretending he had no physical failings – he'd be a laughing stock if he stood next to it when it went on display. So he had the artist killed and sent for another.

The second fellow had heard of the sultan's anger and the subsequent fate of his predecessor, and opted for the warts-and-all approach, making a virtue of the sultan's physical flaws. He depicted the sultan sitting in a chair with his eye-patch and lone leg there for all to see, and leaning slightly forward to accommodate his hump.

When the sultan saw this, he was even more furious. How would that look alongside his ancestors' glorious portraits around the palace? And what would future generations make of such a miserable figure? He was so upset he had that artist killed too.

The next painter the sultan approached was a sly old dog with more suss than a Cockney two-card trickster. 'I know exactly what you want,' he told his ruler.

Three weeks later, he presented his work to the sultan, and it was a model compromise of fact, fiction and vanity. He painted the sultan in heroic pose: on horseback, so his absent leg was not in view; facing forward, in order that his hunch would be invisible; and firing a rifle, with the rangefinder obscuring his missing eye.

trouble *brewing*

A work colleague used to be a foreman down on the Channel Tunnel. He had to interview labourers from all over the place for various jobs on the site.

They had plenty of hod carriers, brickies and plumbers, but were a bit short of qualified fork-lift drivers.

The interviews were being held in a damp shed somewhere under the Channel and the first candidate was a very experienced Irish worker.

The foreman always started off with a fun question. 'Can you make tea?' he began.

'Of course.'

'And can you drive a fork-lift?'

'Jeez,' replied the interviewee, 'how big's the tea pot?'

Other Chunnel stories suggest that despite vehement official denials of the thinness of the rock above the tunnel and likelihood of cracking and a flood disaster, all suppliers of cable and electrical installations used in the project have been asked to make sure their goods are waterproof (!).

Then there's the fact that although there has been a high mortality rate on the Chunnel project, the real toll may be much higher – many of the workers were casual labourers, and no one really kept tabs on how many there were at the beginning and the end.

Oh, and when you ride on the train, don't be surprised if there's a bump halfway across – the French did their tunnelling five feet lower than the British moles, so the tracks didn't meet at the same level. That's why it took so long to complete, but it's all been hushed up.

That's not the only type of underground myth, of course.

danger *down below*

A schoolmate did very well in his exams and left with high hopes. I saw him a couple of weeks back and discovered he'd become a sanitation engineer, so life had gone equally well for both of us. In the course of his work, he often has the unenviable task of inspecting his city's sewers.

Apparently he was on one of his perfumed subterranean walkabouts recently when he came across a chap eating his sandwiches. They were just passing the time of day when a third overalled sewage worker came scuttling round the S-bend. His helmet was askew, and he was brushing himself down and looking over his shoulder the whole while in a fraught fashion.

'What's got the wind up you?' chomped his workmate.

'It was horrible!' gibbered the windy sewerman. 'I was just up a shaft round the corner when of all things a half-dead anaconda dropped on me from above and wrapped itself round me.

'I wouldn't mind,' he continued, 'but it's the third time this month.'

broom *with a view*

A friend of a friend's dad is quite high up in the civil service, not quite a mandarin but certainly more important than a satsuma. Anyways, he recently had to sit in on an interview panel for internal candidates applying for promotion.

The room was as you'd expect – a well-varnished, oak-panelled affair with a single chair placed in front of a long table, behind which sat the six severe interviewers. Most of the prospective candidates were understandably intimidated and meekly entered the room in alphabetical order.

One candidate in particular was especially nervous. He stammered his name, then blushed voluminously and was visibly shaking as the panel set about grilling him.

When the interview was concluded, the bloke stood up, thanked the panel profusely with a frog-in-the-throat voice, and whirled round to leave. After a moment's hesitation he marched decisively to the door and disappeared from the room.

The panel looked at each other and after a few minutes continued the interviews until the end of the session. Then gathering their belongings, they vacated the room, leaving the nervous candidate still cringing in the broom cupboard.

close *calls*

Back in the early eighties British Leyland were experiencing worse than expected sales results from one of their top-flight new models, just launched in Germany. The vehicle in question was the state-of-the-art Triumph Acclaim, produced in a ground-breaking joint venture with the world-beating Japanese.

The car seemed to be doing well everywhere else in Europe and the States; the engineering was faultless, the spec superb for the price, and the fuel economy second to none in its class.

The problem seemed to be a localised one.

The management wracked their brains but couldn't fathom it, until some good new European with a rudimentary grasp of the Teutonic tongue pointed out that it might have something to do with the name: 'Triumph Acclaim' almost literally translates into German as 'Sieg Heil' . . .

A Japanese car company also fell foul of linguistic subtleties when naming their latest sports saloon. As is often the case, they wanted to name it after an animal that embodied the car's virtues. They chose a horse in its prime, for its power, purpose and vitality. But by some quirk of linguistics, when the first sleek black saloon came shimmering off the production line, the glittering chrome badge read 'Starrion', not 'Stallion'.

It was far too expensive to stop the production line, so the name stayed.

Newcastle-upon-Tyne Polytechnic had a dilemma about changing its name on assumption of university status. Other metropolitan polys had opted for simply 'City University of . .' But for some reason this suggestion was deemed inappropriate for Newcastle-upon-Tyne. Perhaps it had something to do with shortening the name to initials . . .

so *re-spectacle*

An old friend's mum works in the local hairdressers'. Once a week they have OAP specials when old fellas can come and have their tresses trimmed at reduced rates.

Apparently, one day a regular customer, a respectable elderly gent in his early seventies, settled down in the chair for his usual short back and sides. (In truth, he had such a thin thatch it was barely worth his bus fare, but he enjoyed the company in the queue.)

His usual barber was away in Tenerife, so one of the

young trainee girls happily volunteered for the job. She was slightly disconcerted when she caught the old gent squinting at her bending over the sink.

But she shrugged it off, and began merrily snipping away and wittering mindlessly about the weather and TV soaps.

A little later, mid snip, the trainee happened to glance down and noticed some disconcerting movement beneath the protective nylon cape she'd put round the old chap. At first she tried to carry on regardless, ignoring his fixed expression.

But again the rhythmic motion caught her eye.

Fetching the old gent a hefty clout, she bawled, 'Cut that out, you dirty old sod!'

'B–but I'm only cleaning these,' the stunned old gent replied, lifting the cape to reveal his polished spectacles.

mythellaneous

Jobs

✳ Colour-blind people make better bomber pilots, because they're not deceived by camouflage

✳ Undercover police often pose as artists. You can 'easely' spot them by how dodgy the pictures are

✳ Nuclear bomber pilots have to wear an eye-patch so that in the event of an atomic flash, one eye can still see

✳ The Bank of England now employs origami experts to check new notes can't be folded in a way that puts the Queen into obscene poses

✳ In the First World War, soldiers desperate to be invalided out and sent home performed handstands in the trenches, with their feet poking over the top, hoping they would be shot

✳ Dead sailors fished out of the briny by coastguards are often found to have their trouser zipper undone. It's called 'FOA' – Flies Open on Arrival – in the trade

✳ Prostitutes join the US Navy as female sailors, enrol on aircraft carriers and make a fortune, sending their earnings back home in conspicuous packages – that's how they get found out

✳ Russian prostitutes accept share certificates as payment for services rendered

wan*ted*

As part of our mission to collate all the world's greatest urban myths, we invite readers who would like to share their best stories with us to write them down and kindly send them to:

> **Phil Healey and Rick Glanvill**
> **Planet X**
> **97 St John's Street**
> **London EC1M 4AS**

We are particularly interested in apocryphal stories connected with occupations like the emergency services, the armed forces and social work, and in urban legends from around the globe, but all contributions are much appreciated.